iPhone 14 Seniors Guide:

Unlock the Wonders of Your iPhone 14 with Our Simple Guide. Discover Essential Tips & Tricks for Seniors to Maximize Your Device's Potential Easily.

Evan MacIntyre

Table Of Contents

Introduction

Welcome to Your iPhone 14!

Congratulations on your new iPhone 14! Whether you're upgrading from a previous model or diving into the world of smartphones for the first time, this guide is your companion on a journey through innovation, convenience, and connectivity. The iPhone 14 represents a significant leap forward in technology, designed to enhance your communication and entertainment experiences while ensuring simplicity and ease of use.

As you unbox your iPhone 14, you might first notice its sleek design—the elegant contours and the sophisticated finish that Apple is renowned for. But the true beauty of your iPhone lies not just in its appearance but in its functionality. From the moment you power on your device, you're greeted by a vibrant display that promises a world of possibilities waiting at your fingertips.

Starting with the basics, the iPhone 14 comes equipped with a user-friendly interface that caters to users of all ages and tech-savviness. The touchscreen is responsive and intuitive, allowing you to navigate through apps and settings with ease. You might find yourself swiping through pages of apps, marveling at the fluidity with which the device responds to your touch.

Understanding the core functions of your iPhone is paramount to enjoying all its features. The iPhone 14 simplifies communication, allowing you to connect with family and friends across the globe in various ways. Whether it's a traditional phone call, a video chat via FaceTime, or a text message, your iPhone facilitates these interactions with a few simple taps.

Photography enthusiasts will appreciate the advanced camera system on the iPhone 14, which captures images in stunning clarity and vibrant colors. Whether you're photographing a family gathering or documenting your travels, the iPhone 14 makes it easy to snap professional-quality photos without needing to be a professional photographer.

But the iPhone 14 is more than just a tool for communication and photography; it's a gateway to a world of entertainment. The App Store offers millions of apps to explore, ranging from games and social media platforms to educational tools and health-related resources. Whatever your interests, there's an app on the iPhone 14 that can enhance your daily life or help you dive into new hobbies.

Safety and security are paramount in the digital age, and the iPhone 14 is equipped with state-of-the-art security features to protect your personal information. From Face ID technology that lets you unlock your phone just by looking at it to advanced encryption methods that safeguard your data, you can use your iPhone with the confidence that your privacy is protected.

For those new to smartphones or upgrading from older models, the learning curve can seem daunting. However, the iPhone 14 is designed to be accessible. Its settings menu is straightforward, allowing you to customize your device to suit your preferences without feeling overwhelmed. Accessibility features are robust, offering options like VoiceOver for those who need audio feedback, or larger text sizes for easier reading.

As you begin to explore your iPhone 14, remember that it is designed to adapt to your needs. The more you use it, the better it understands your preferences, making your digital experience smoother and more personalized. Your iPhone can schedule reminders, suggest apps based on your usage patterns, and even recommend adjustments to settings to optimize battery life and functionality.

Embracing your iPhone 14 is about more than just keeping up with technology—it's about making it a seamless part of your life. Whether it's setting up daily alarms, receiving news updates, or controlling smart home devices, your iPhone becomes a central hub for your day-to-day activities. With each tap, swipe, and press, you'll find more ways that your iPhone 14 can help you stay organized, connected, and entertained.

Welcome aboard, and enjoy your new iPhone 14, a device that isn't just smart, but thoughtful, bringing technology and people together in a way that is accessible and enjoyable for everyone. As you continue to explore, remember that this guide is here to help you navigate the exciting features of your iPhone 14, ensuring that you make the most out of your new digital companion.

Meet Your Guide: Getting Started with the Basics

Embarking on the journey of mastering your new iPhone 14, it's crucial to have a reliable guide by your side. This chapter is designed to be that guide, helping you navigate the initial steps of getting to know your device. As we walk through these fundamentals, you'll find that your iPhone is more than just a piece of technology; it's a portal to new experiences, streamlined through intuitive design and user-focused features.

The beauty of the iPhone 14 lies in its simplicity. Apple has always aimed to create devices that are both powerful and easy to use, and your new iPhone is no exception. From the moment you turn on your device, you're guided through a seamless setup process. This initial setup is your first step toward personalizing your iPhone, from choosing your language to setting up Wi-Fi and entering your Apple ID. Each step is presented in a clear, easy-to-understand manner, ensuring you feel confident as you proceed.

Once your iPhone is set up, the real exploration begins. The home screen is your starting point, a gateway to everything your iPhone can do. Here, you'll find pre-installed apps like Messages, Photos, and Mail, arranged in a grid that is navigable with a simple swipe of your finger. This might seem straightforward, but the real magic happens as you start interacting with these apps. Each one opens up a new world of possibilities—communicating with loved ones, capturing and sharing memories, and managing your daily tasks.

Understanding how to navigate your iPhone is key. The touch interface of the iPhone 14 is designed to respond to various gestures—taps, swipes, and pinches—all of which become second nature with a little practice. These gestures make navigating your iPhone feel natural, almost as if the device is an extension of yourself. For instance, swiping down from the top of the screen reveals the notification center, a convenient place to see all your recent messages, alerts, and updates at a glance.

Another fundamental aspect of getting started with your iPhone is understanding the Control Center. Accessed by swiping down from the upper right corner of the screen, the Control Center is a powerful tool for quickly toggling settings like Wi-Fi, Bluetooth, and airplane mode. It also gives you easy access to key utilities such as the flashlight, calculator, and camera. Learning how to customize the Control Center to fit your needs can significantly enhance your efficiency and enjoyment in using your iPhone.

Perhaps one of the most critical steps in getting started with your iPhone is familiarizing yourself with the Settings app. This central hub allows you to control everything from screen brightness and wallpaper to privacy settings and passwords. While it might seem daunting at first, spending time exploring the Settings app can empower you to tailor your device to your exact preferences, enhancing both functionality and security.

Your iPhone is also equipped with Siri, Apple's voice-activated assistant. Learning to use Siri can simplify tasks like sending messages, setting reminders, or getting directions, all without lifting a finger. Engaging with Siri isn't just about giving commands; it's about interacting with an assistant who can learn from and adapt to your preferences, making everyday tasks easier and more personalized.

As you continue to explore, you'll discover that your iPhone is a hub for accessibility. With features designed to assist users with various needs, such as VoiceOver for the visually impaired, or hearing aids compatibility, your device ensures that technology is accessible to all. These features show Apple's commitment to inclusivity, making sure that everyone can take full advantage of their technology.

In mastering the basics of your iPhone 14, remember that this device is designed to work for you. It's built to adapt to your lifestyle, whether you're connecting with family, managing your professional life, or exploring new hobbies through apps. Each feature has been thoughtfully designed to enhance your interactions and simplify your day.

As we wrap up this introduction to the basics, it's clear that your journey with the iPhone 14 is just beginning. With each feature you explore and every app you open, you'll uncover more ways to make your iPhone a valuable part of your daily life. So, take your time, explore at your own pace, and remember: your iPhone is more than just a tool—it's your partner in navigating the digital world. Welcome to a new chapter of convenience, connection, and discovery.

Chapter 1: Getting to Know Your iPhone 14

Embark on a journey to unlock the full potential of your iPhone 14 by delving into its intricacies and features. This chapter is your gateway to understanding the essentials of your device, from its sleek design to the personalized settings that make your iPhone truly yours. We will explore the physical features that define the iPhone 14's sophisticated engineering, navigate through the intuitive home screen, harness the power of the Control Center, and delve into how to customize settings to suit your preferences and lifestyle. Each section is designed to provide you with a comprehensive understanding of your device, ensuring that you are equipped to use your iPhone 14 to its fullest capability.

Understanding Your iPhone's Physical Features

As you hold your iPhone 14 for the first time, you might marvel at its sleek design. This device is not just a phone; it's a carefully crafted piece of technology that combines aesthetics with functionality. The iPhone 14's physical features are designed to provide comfort and convenience, ensuring that every interaction enhances your experience.

The first thing you'll notice is the iPhone 14's outer frame, made from aerospace-grade aluminum, which not only gives it a modern look but also makes it durable. The front and back are covered with a special Ceramic Shield, significantly tougher than any smartphone glass, offering increased resistance to drops and scratches. This durability means your device is equipped to handle the rigors of everyday use while maintaining its elegant appearance.

Turning the device over in your hands, you will feel the smoothness of its edges, designed to fit comfortably in your palm. The arrangement of the buttons is intuitive; on the right side, you'll find the power button, which also serves as a lock screen button. On the left, there are the volume controls and the ring/silent switch, a staple in iPhone design that allows you to quickly silence your phone without having to unlock it.

One of the most significant features is the iPhone 14's camera system. On the back, you'll see the advanced dual-camera setup housed in a precise alignment. This setup includes a 12-megapixel wide camera and a 12-megapixel ultra-wide camera, designed to capture stunning photos and videos in high definition. The front camera is no less impressive, with a TrueDepth camera system that enables Face ID, allowing you to unlock your phone simply by looking at it.

At the bottom of the iPhone, the charging port and speakers are neatly integrated. The iPhone 14 supports MagSafe technology, which improves wireless charging and allows for the attachment of various accessories like wallets and cases magnetically. This feature not only enhances the functionality but also the versatility of your iPhone.

Lastly, the color options for the iPhone 14 are both vibrant and subdued, catering to a variety of tastes. Whether you prefer the classic elegance of Midnight or the boldness of Product(RED), there is a color that matches your personal style. In grasping the physical aspects of your iPhone 14, you begin to appreciate the thought and craftsmanship that went into its design. Each element is not just for aesthetic appeal but serves a practical purpose, ensuring that your device is as user-friendly as it is technologically advanced. As you familiarize yourself with these features, you start to realize the capability at your fingertips, ready to explore more of what your iPhone can do in the chapters to come.

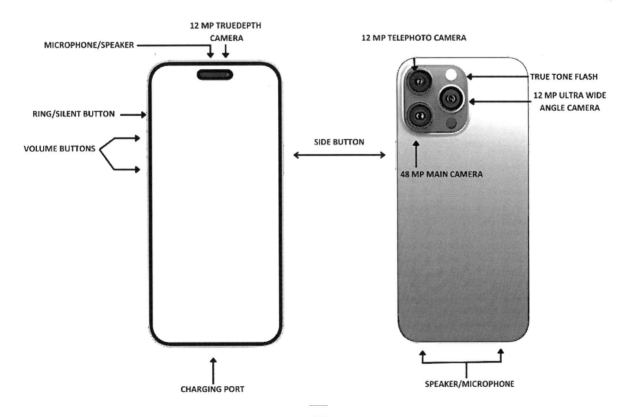

Navigating the Home Screen

The home screen of your iPhone 14 is the starting point of your digital journey, a gateway to all the capabilities and features your phone has to offer. It's designed to be intuitive, making it easy for users of all ages to navigate and access their apps and settings with minimal effort. Understanding how to effectively maneuver through this digital landscape will unlock the full potential of your device.

When you first unlock your iPhone, you're greeted by the home screen, a display of colorful icons representing different apps. These icons are your immediate touchpoints to everything from your camera and photo library to your messages and favorite games. Apple has refined the art of simplicity in design, ensuring that these icons are arranged in a grid that is easy to understand and operate. You can swipe left or right to view additional pages of apps, each swipe bringing you a new set of options.

The home screen is more than just a static display; it's customizable to suit your personal preferences and lifestyle. If you find yourself frequently using certain apps, you can arrange your home screen to keep these apps within easy reach. By simply pressing and holding an app icon, you enter the edit mode where you can drag and rearrange icons. This allows you to place your most-used apps on the first page, or group similar apps into folders, creating a truly tailored user experience.

At the bottom of the home screen, you'll find the dock, a special area that holds up to four apps. These remain visible across all home screen pages, providing quick access to the tools you use most frequently. Many people choose to place phone, message, email, and music apps here, but you can customize this to include any apps you prefer, from social media to health-tracking.

Beyond the visible apps, the home screen on the iPhone 14 offers deeper integrations with its ecosystem. A simple swipe down from the middle of the screen brings up the Spotlight search, a powerful tool that not only helps you find apps and contacts but also offers suggestions based on your usage patterns. It's a quick way to access not just apps but also in-app content without having to navigate through multiple screens.

Swiping right from the main home screen page reveals the Today View, a customizable area where you can add widgets—mini-applications that display condensed information from apps you use frequently. Whether it's your calendar, weather updates, or fitness activity, widgets provide a snapshot of app data at a glance. This integration turns your home screen into a dynamic space that not only launches apps but also provides real-time information tailored to your needs.

As you familiarize yourself with navigating the home screen of your iPhone 14, you'll discover the thoughtfulness Apple has put into every design decision. From the tactile feedback of pressing an app icon to the fluid animation that accompanies each swipe, every detail is crafted to enhance your interaction with your device. This is where your comfort with the iPhone begins and grows, as each interaction becomes more intuitive, making your daily digital interactions second nature.

Exploring the Control Center

The Control Center on your iPhone 14 is a hub of utility, designed to provide quick access to frequently used controls and settings. It's a feature that enhances your phone's usability, allowing you to quickly adjust settings without digging through menus or leaving the app you're currently using. This seamless integration of functionality is key to a streamlined, efficient user experience, particularly important in today's fast-paced world.

Accessing the Control Center is effortless; a simple swipe down from the top-right corner of your screen—whether your phone is locked or in use—reveals a palette of icons and sliders. This gesture-based access is designed to feel intuitive, mirroring the natural motions you might already be accustomed to on your device. Once open, the Control Center's sleek, semi-transparent background blends with whatever is on your screen, ensuring that usability doesn't come at the expense of aesthetics.

The layout of the Control Center is thoughtfully organized to put the most essential toggles at your fingertips. Wi-Fi, Bluetooth, and Airplane Mode are prominently placed, allowing you to quickly connect or disconnect from networks or devices. The brightness and volume sliders offer tactile control over your phone's audio and visual settings, responsive and satisfying to adjust, reflecting Apple's focus on ensuring a tactile interface.

Moreover, the Control Center is customizable—a feature that many iPhone users might not initially explore. By going into the Settings app, you can choose which controls appear and how they are arranged. This customization makes your Control Center uniquely yours, tailored to fit the tools you use most. Whether it's adding shortcuts for the flashlight and calculator or incorporating controls for home automation via HomeKit, these adjustments make your device feel even more personal and efficient.

Another innovative feature within the Control Center is the inclusion of contextual controls like screen recording and Do Not Disturb. These features illustrate the dynamic nature of iPhone software, where even supplementary functions are designed to enhance your interaction with the device. Screen recording, for example, allows you to capture what happens on your screen live—useful for everything from creating tutorials to saving memorable gameplay.

The Control Center also extends its functionality with quick access to camera and torch, which are indispensable tools for many users. The ease with which you can turn on the torch or quickly switch to camera mode without unlocking your phone or navigating through apps underscores the iPhone's commitment to convenience and accessibility.

In essence, the Control Center is a reflection of the philosophy behind the iPhone 14: to create a device that is powerful, yet simple enough for anyone to use. It's a perfect example of how modern technology can be made user-friendly without sacrificing capability or performance. As you become more familiar with the Control Center, you'll appreciate not just the access it provides but also the way it enhances your overall interaction with your iPhone, making daily

LOCK SCREEN   **CONTROL CENTRE**   **QUICK CONNECTIONS**

SWIPE DOWN

PRESS DOWN

Customizing Your Settings

Delving into the Settings of your iPhone 14 unveils a world where you can tailor each aspect of your device to your personal preferences and lifestyle. This customization not only enhances your user experience by making your device more intuitive and enjoyable to use but also empowers you to control your digital environment according to your unique needs and habits.

The Settings menu of the iPhone 14 acts as the command center for your device, where you can modify features ranging from the network and connectivity to sounds and display settings. This comprehensive hub ensures that you can adjust nearly every facet of your phone's functionality, from the mundane to the complex, with a few taps.

When you first visit the Settings app, you might feel overwhelmed by the variety of options available. However, these settings are thoughtfully organized into clear categories, making it easy to navigate and find the specific setting you wish to adjust. For example, if you want to change how notifications are displayed or set which apps can send you alerts, the Notifications section provides you with detailed control over these aspects.

One of the most commonly customized features is the display settings. Here, you can adjust the brightness and color balance, which can help in reducing eye strain during extended use. The Night Shift mode, which alters the screen's color temperature during evening hours to aid in better sleep, is a favored feature for many users. Furthermore, if you prefer larger text for easier reading, you can change text size and boldness to make everything from emails to app icons more legible.

Privacy settings are another crucial area within the Settings app. Your iPhone 14 comes equipped with numerous options to protect your personal information. From deciding which apps can access your location to setting up Face ID and passcodes, these tools are designed to give you peace of mind knowing that your data is secure. You can also manage settings for Safari to limit tracking, control which apps have access to your camera and microphone, and much more.

Another significant area of customization involves sound and haptics. In this menu, you can tailor how your device reacts to touches and notifications. Whether it's setting the ringtone, adjusting the volume limits, or choosing the vibration patterns for different kinds of alerts, these settings allow you to personalize how you interact with your device audibly and tactilely.

Moreover, for those who utilize their iPhone for work and personal life, the Focus mode, accessible through the settings, allows you to set boundaries on your device. By customizing Focus settings, you can filter notifications based on what you are currently doing—be it working, driving, or spending time with family—ensuring that you can concentrate without unnecessary distractions.

Conclusion to Chapter 1: Getting to Know Your iPhone 14

As we conclude this chapter, you should now feel more confident and familiar with your iPhone 14. You've learned about its physical attributes, discovered how to navigate the essential interfaces, and explored the depth of customization available at your fingertips. With this knowledge, you're well on your way to mastering your device, making it a valuable tool in your daily life. Remember, the iPhone 14 is designed not just for communication but as an extension of your personal and professional life. Continue to explore and experiment with the settings and features discussed, as familiarity will enhance your experience and proficiency. Your journey with the iPhone 14 is just beginning, and the possibilities are endless.

Chapter 2: Making Calls and Sending Messages

In today's connected world, your iPhone 14 serves as more than just a device; it's a lifeline to the world around you. This chapter delves into the various ways the iPhone 14 facilitates communication, from traditional phone calls and text messaging to modern video calls and the use of diverse third-party apps. We begin by exploring the basic yet crucial functionalities of making and receiving calls, offering insights into both the simplicity and sophistication of your device. We then transition to the nuances of sending and receiving text messages, followed by the dynamic world of FaceTime for video interactions. Finally, we will expand our scope to include a variety of other communication apps available through the App Store, showcasing the iPhone's versatility in adapting to all your communication needs.

Making and Receiving Calls

The primary function of any phone is to enable communication, and your iPhone 14 excels at this fundamental task with unparalleled ease and clarity. Making and receiving calls on your iPhone is a seamless process, designed to connect you with others without the hassle of navigating through complicated menus or settings. Let's explore how the iPhone 14 simplifies this essential communication function.

When you're ready to make a call, the Phone app, represented by the iconic green icon, is your starting point. Opening this app reveals a keypad, allowing you to dial a number directly. For added convenience, your iPhone 14 is smart enough to suggest numbers based on your previous calls, so reaching your frequent contacts is faster than ever. Additionally, you can access your contact list through the Contacts tab within the same app, making it simple to call family, friends, or coworkers with just a tap.

Receiving calls on your iPhone 14 is just as user-friendly. Whether your phone is locked or in use, an incoming call displays the caller's name, number, and photo if they are saved in your contacts. You can easily accept the call with a swipe or dismiss it if you're unavailable, options that are intuitively presented. Moreover, should you decide to decline a call, your iPhone offers quick responses that you can send as text messages, explaining why you can't answer. This feature is particularly useful during meetings or when you are otherwise engaged.

The iPhone 14 also supports voice-over LTE (VoLTE) and Wi-Fi calling, features that enhance call quality and reliability. VoLTE offers clearer audio, making conversations sound more natural, while Wi-Fi calling is an excellent option in areas with poor cellular reception, as it allows calls to be made over a Wi-Fi network instead of a cellular network. This ensures that you remain connected even in challenging conditions.

Customizing your call settings further enhances the calling experience. Your iPhone allows you to set up call forwarding, caller ID, and block numbers directly from the settings menu. This level of customization not only makes your communication more secure but also more personalized, as you can manage who can reach you and when.

In addition to these practical aspects, the iPhone 14 offers various ringtones and vibration patterns that can be assigned to specific contacts. This personalization allows you to know who is calling without needing to look at your device, a convenience that simplifies your daily interactions.

Overall, making and receiving calls with your iPhone 14 is a straightforward and enriched experience. The integration of advanced technology and user-friendly design ensures that connecting with others is a pleasure, not a chore. As you continue to use your iPhone, you'll discover more nuances and features that make everyday communications smoother and more enjoyable, reinforcing the iPhone's status as a top-tier communication tool.

Sending and Receiving Text Messages

Text messaging is a pivotal form of communication in today's digital world, and your iPhone 14 makes this essential activity effortless and engaging. With the Messages app, your device provides a powerful platform for not only sending and receiving texts but also for making your conversations lively and interactive with features like Memoji and iMessage effects. This chapter delves into the intuitive functionality of the Messages app, ensuring that your texting experience is as rich and enjoyable as it is straightforward.

Upon opening the Messages app, you are greeted by a clean, user-friendly interface. Conversations are neatly organized, making it easy to find ongoing chats or start new ones. To compose a message, simply tap the compose button, and type the contact name or number. The smart predictive text feature helps by suggesting words as you type, reducing your typing time and improving accuracy.

Receiving messages is just as seamless. Notifications appear on your lock screen or as banners at the top of your screen when the device is in use. You can tap these notifications to go directly to the message, or swipe to manage notification settings quickly. For privacy, you can adjust settings to hide message previews from the lock screen.

The real charm of the iPhone's messaging capabilities lies in its advanced features. iMessage, Apple's messaging service, enables you to send text messages, photos, videos, and voice messages over Wi-Fi or cellular data to other Apple devices without incurring SMS fees. Messages sent via iMessage appear in blue bubbles, whereas regular SMS messages appear in green. This distinction helps you understand immediately whether you are using iMessage or SMS—a useful feature for managing potential data usage.

iMessage also supports features like read receipts and typing indicators, which can be toggled on or off in the Settings app. These features let you see when the recipient has read your message or is typing a response, enhancing the interactive experience of your conversations.

Another exciting feature is the ability to react to messages with Tapbacks—quick responses like a thumbs up or a heart—and the use of Digital Touch, which lets you send sketches, taps, or even your heartbeat. These playful interactions add a personal touch to your conversations, making them more expressive and fun.

For those who enjoy more visual communication, the Messages app integrates seamlessly with the camera and photo library, allowing you to share images and videos directly in your conversations. Enhancements like photo filters, annotation tools, and the option to create and send GIFs make sharing content simple and enjoyable.

Moreover, Apple's commitment to accessibility is evident in the Messages app through features like predictive text and voice-to-text capabilities, which significantly aid users with different abilities in crafting their messages.

In summary, the Messages app on your iPhone 14 is much more than a tool for sending texts. It's a dynamic platform that enhances how you connect with friends and family, blending simplicity with advanced messaging technology to create a truly enriched communication experience. As you continue to explore these features, you'll find yourself engaging in conversations that are not only meaningful but also delightfully interactive.

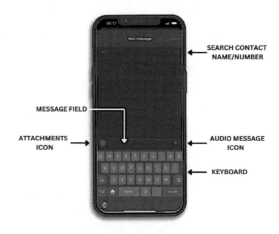

Using FaceTime for Video Calls

FaceTime, Apple's proprietary video calling app, has revolutionized the way people connect visually with family, friends, and colleagues around the world. Your iPhone 14 harnesses the power of this app to deliver high-quality video calls that are not only clear but also secure, thanks to end-to-end encryption. This section explores how to make the most of FaceTime, enhancing your communication with a personal touch.

The simplicity of FaceTime is one of its most appealing features. To start a video call, simply open the FaceTime app and enter the Apple ID or phone number of the person you want to call, or select their name from your contacts. A tap on the video icon initiates the call. If the person is available, you'll soon see them on your screen, framed within a user interface that is unobtrusive yet functional, allowing you to focus on the conversation.

FaceTime's integration with your iPhone 14's camera and microphone is seamless, providing a video and audio quality that feels natural and engaging. The app utilizes the front-facing TrueDepth camera, which supports advanced image stabilization and Portrait mode, blurring the background and keeping the focus sharply on you. This feature is particularly useful in professional settings or in conversations where you want to ensure the emphasis remains on the speaker.

The responsiveness of FaceTime is noteworthy. As network conditions change during a call, the app adjusts the video resolution and bitrate in real-time to maintain call quality without dropping the connection. This adaptability makes FaceTime reliable in a variety of situations, whether you're calling from a bustling airport lounge or a quiet room at home.

For those with family or friends abroad, FaceTime is indispensable. Unlike traditional international calls, FaceTime uses your data plan or Wi-Fi network, thus avoiding international calling fees. This makes it an economical choice for long-distance relationships, allowing you to stay visually connected with loved ones without concern for cost.

Moreover, FaceTime supports group calls, making it a fantastic tool for coordinating family get-togethers or business meetings. You can add multiple people to a FaceTime call, turning a regular video call into a group hangout where everyone can catch up, share news, or collaborate on projects. The app dynamically adjusts the screen to feature the person speaking, making conversations flow more naturally and reducing the chaos often associated with group calls.

FaceTime also offers features like 'FaceTime links', which you can create ahead of a scheduled call and share via email or messages, making it easier to manage invitations and schedules. This feature extends the functionality of FaceTime, integrating it more deeply into your planning and communication strategies.

In essence, FaceTime on your iPhone 14 is more than just a video calling application—it is a robust tool for personal and professional communication that bridges distances with a touch of immediacy and intimacy not found in voice calls alone. As you use FaceTime more frequently, you'll discover its potential not just as a tool for occasional calls but as a staple of everyday communication, enriching your connections and making your interactions more memorable.

Exploring Other Communication Apps

While the iPhone 14 provides robust native applications for calling and messaging, such as the Phone and Messages apps, and FaceTime for video calls, the App Store offers a treasure trove of additional communication apps designed to meet diverse needs and preferences. These apps extend the functionality of your device, allowing for innovative ways to stay connected, share experiences, and even manage professional communications more effectively.

One of the most popular types of communication apps available on the App Store is instant messaging apps. Applications like WhatsApp, Telegram, and Signal provide rich messaging features including text, voice messages, video calls, and file sharing, all secured with end-to-end encryption. These apps are particularly valuable for users who communicate internationally, as they use an internet connection rather than cellular plans, thereby reducing costs and bypassing international barriers.

Social media platforms, which often integrate direct messaging features, represent another category of communication apps. Apps like Instagram, Facebook, and Twitter not only allow users to share updates and media with a broad audience but also offer private messaging functionalities. These platforms make it possible to connect with friends, family, and followers in a multifaceted way that goes beyond traditional messaging, integrating elements of social interaction and media sharing.

For professional communication, apps like Slack and Microsoft Teams have become indispensable in many business environments. These apps provide comprehensive communication solutions that include chat, voice and video calls, and collaboration tools all in one platform. They are designed to enhance productivity by centralizing communication, making it easier to manage tasks, share files, and maintain transparency with colleagues, regardless of location.

Another innovative communication option is voice over IP (VoIP) apps such as Skype and Google Voice. These services offer voice calls, video calls, and messaging across a range of devices, using the internet to transmit data. This technology makes these apps ideal for business calls and personal chats, especially for contacting people who do not use smartphones, as many VoIP services offer calls to landlines and mobile phones at competitive rates.

Lastly, specialized communication apps cater to niche needs. For example, Discord is popular among gamers for its robust community features and support for large group communications, while dating apps like Tinder and Bumble feature messaging as a core part of their user interaction.

Conclusion to Chapter 2: Making Calls and Sending Messages

As we conclude this exploration of the communication capabilities of your iPhone 14, you are now equipped with the knowledge to utilize your device's full potential in keeping you connected with others. Whether it's through a simple phone call, a message, a face-to-face video chat via FaceTime, or through any of the numerous other communication apps available, your iPhone 14 is an indispensable tool in your daily interactions. Each section of this chapter has been designed to not only introduce these features but also to demonstrate how they can be customized and integrated into your lifestyle. As you continue to communicate using your iPhone, remember that each feature is crafted to enhance your experience and connectivity, ensuring that no matter where you are, your iPhone 14 keeps you in touch with what matters most.

Chapter 3: Exploring Essential Apps

Welcome to the digital hub of your iPhone 14, where the essential apps reside that make your device incredibly powerful and versatile. In this chapter, we delve into the core applications that enhance the functionality of your iPhone, making everyday tasks simpler and more intuitive. We begin by understanding the App Store, your gateway to countless apps tailored to suit any need or interest. Next, we explore Safari, the robust web browser designed for seamless browsing and privacy. We'll also cover the Mail app, which streamlines your email management with efficiency and ease. Lastly, we turn our attention to Maps, a comprehensive navigation tool that guides you from point A to point B with precision. Each section is crafted to help you leverage these applications to their fullest, enriching your experience with your iPhone 14.

Understanding the App Store

The App Store is the heart of software discovery and installation for your iPhone 14, acting as a central marketplace where you can explore, download, and manage applications that enhance the functionality of your device. Whether you're looking for tools to increase productivity, games to entertain, or resources to improve your daily life, the App Store is your gateway to a vast world of apps designed to suit a variety of needs and preferences.

When you launch the App Store on your iPhone 14, you're welcomed by a user-friendly interface that is both intuitive and inviting. The homepage itself is a curated experience, showcasing app recommendations, trending searches, and new releases tailored to your preferences and previous app interactions. This personalized approach helps streamline your search for new apps by highlighting those that are likely to be of most interest to you.

Navigating the App Store is a seamless experience, with the interface divided into several key sections: 'Today', 'Games', 'Apps', and 'Updates'. Each tab offers a unique perspective on the available apps. The 'Today' tab, for example, features daily stories, tips, and collections that introduce you to new and noteworthy apps and games, enriching your understanding of what your iPhone 14 can do. The 'Games' and 'Apps' tabs are specifically categorized to help users drill down into their areas of interest, from entertainment to lifestyle to education, ensuring you find exactly what you need.

One of the most beneficial features of the App Store is its focus on security and quality. Every app on the App Store is reviewed by Apple to ensure it meets a high standard of quality and security, providing you with confidence in the downloads you choose. This review process includes an evaluation of the app's functionality, its adherence to privacy policies, and its overall reliability, protecting users from malicious software and ensuring a trustworthy user experience.

The search functionality within the App Store is robust, equipped with advanced algorithms that help predict and suggest search terms, making the discovery process more efficient. Once you find an app that interests you, the App Store provides detailed information, including developer descriptions, user reviews, and ratings. This information is crucial in helping you make informed decisions about whether an app suits your needs.

Furthermore, the App Store is not just about discovering new apps but also managing the ones you already have. The 'Updates' tab displays updates available for your installed apps, ensuring you always have the latest features and security enhancements. This aspect of the App Store is essential for maintaining the apps on your iPhone 14, keeping them up-to-date and functioning optimally.

In conclusion, the App Store on your iPhone 14 is much more than a simple digital store—it's a comprehensive platform for app discovery and management. It empowers you to customize your device in infinitely personal ways, enhancing your interaction with your iPhone 14 through applications that cater to every aspect of your life. As you explore the App Store, each app you download transforms your iPhone from a mere communication device into a personalized tool crafted to your lifestyle and needs.

Exploring Safari for Web Browsing

Safari, the default web browser on your iPhone 14, is a gateway to the vast world of the internet. Engineered for speed, efficiency, and user safety, Safari offers a seamless browsing experience that makes it simple to explore, discover, and manage the wealth of information available online. As we delve into the capabilities of Safari, you will learn how to make the most of this powerful tool to enhance your web interactions.

Upon opening Safari, you are greeted with a clean, streamlined interface designed for ease of use. The search bar at the top doubles as a place to type URLs and search queries, powered by Apple's chosen search engine. Below this, your frequently visited sites appear as icons, providing quick access to your favorite web pages. This design not only speeds up navigation but also makes it more intuitive.

One of Safari's standout features is its speed. Optimized to work with the advanced hardware of the iPhone 14, Safari loads pages swiftly, even those rich in media and interactive elements. This responsiveness ensures that your browsing experience is not only fast but also enjoyable, free from the frustrations of slow page loads.

Privacy is a cornerstone of Safari's design. The browser incorporates advanced features to protect your online activities from unwanted tracking and intrusion. Intelligent Tracking Prevention (ITP) uses machine learning to identify advertisers and others who track your online behavior, and removes the cross-site tracking data they leave behind. This means that your browsing habits remain private, and the ads you see are less likely to be tailored by tracking your activity across different sites.

Safari also supports a range of user-friendly features that enhance your browsing experience. The Reader mode strips away clutter like ads and pop-ups from articles, presenting you with just the text and essential images, making for a cleaner and more focused reading experience. Moreover, you can easily save articles to your Reading List to access later, even offline, or add them to your bookmarks for repeated access.

Tab management in Safari is straightforward and effective. You can open new tabs with a tap, switch between them with a swipe, and close them by tapping the small 'x' on the tab. For those who browse with many tabs open, the ability to organize them into groups makes managing multiple topics and tasks easier than ever.

Safari's integration with the broader Apple ecosystem enhances its utility. For example, if you also use Safari on your Mac, iCloud can sync your tabs, bookmarks, and reading list across devices. This means you can start reading an article on your iPhone and finish it on your Mac without missing a beat.

In essence, Safari on your iPhone 14 is more than just a tool for accessing the web—it is a comprehensive platform that supports a wide range of browsing activities, from casual surfing to intense research. Its combination of speed, simplicity, and security ensures that your online experiences are efficient, enjoyable, and private, empowering you to use the internet in ways that suit your needs and preferences perfectly.

TAP ON SAFARI ICON

TAP ON SEARCH BAR AND TYPE

TAP ON GO TO SEARCH

Managing Your Email with the Mail App

Email remains a cornerstone of digital communication, whether it's for personal correspondences, professional engagements, or managing subscriptions and notifications. The Mail app on your iPhone 14 is designed to handle your email needs with proficiency and ease, integrating seamlessly into your daily life to ensure you stay connected and organized.

The Mail app on the iPhone 14 excels in its simplicity and functionality. Opening the app, you are greeted by an inbox categorized by threads, making it easier to follow conversations without getting lost in individual messages. This threaded view can be toggled off if you prefer to see each email separately. The design is intuitive, allowing for quick navigation between multiple accounts, should you use more than one for different aspects of your life.

One of the key features of the Mail app is its powerful search functionality. You can quickly find emails by sender, subject, or even a keyword within the email content. This is particularly useful when you need to reference old correspondences or track down specific attachments. The search capabilities are bolstered by the app's ability to index and retrieve information rapidly, a testament to the sophisticated engineering behind the iPhone 14.

Customization is another strength of the Mail app. It allows you to tailor the settings to fit your preferences, from notification alerts to swipe gestures. For instance, you can set the swipe gestures to either delete, archive, move, or mark emails as read or unread, providing a faster way to manage your inbox directly from the main screen. Additionally, you can filter emails to show only unread messages, flagged emails, messages with attachments, or VIP emails, which simplifies navigating a busy inbox.

Security and privacy are paramount in Apple's design philosophy, and the Mail app is no exception. It uses advanced encryption to protect your emails, ensuring that what you send and receive remains confidential. Furthermore, Apple respects your privacy by not scanning your email content for advertising purposes, a commitment that distinguishes it from some other technology providers.

For those who manage multiple email accounts from different providers, the Mail app supports a variety of email services, including iCloud, Gmail, Outlook, Yahoo, and more. This multi-account support is handled elegantly within the app, allowing you to access all your emails in one place without needing to log in and out.

The Mail app also integrates with other native apps like Calendar and Contacts, offering a holistic experience. For example, when you receive an email containing a date or an invitation, the Mail app can suggest adding this event directly to your Calendar. Similarly, if an email comes from a new contact, you can add this person to your Contacts directly from the Mail app.

In essence, the Mail app on your iPhone 14 is a robust tool designed not just for reading and sending emails but for enhancing how you organize, search, and interact with your digital communications. It stands as a testament to Apple's commitment to creating integrated, user-friendly technologies that support the dynamic lives of its users. With each update and iteration, the Mail app continues to evolve, consistently improving to meet the changing needs of modern email communication.

Using Maps for Navigation

The Maps app on your iPhone 14 is not just a tool for finding your way around; it's a comprehensive navigation assistant designed to make your journeys smoother and more efficient. Whether you're exploring a new city, searching for a local restaurant, or planning a road trip, the Maps app provides detailed, user-friendly guidance that helps you navigate with confidence.

When you open the Maps app, you're presented with a clean, intuitive interface that displays your current location on a detailed map. The search bar at the top allows you to quickly find destinations, businesses, and points of interest. As you type, the app suggests locations based on your current location and search history, making it easier to find what you need swiftly.

One of the standout features of the Maps app is its integration with real-time traffic data. When planning a route, the app not only suggests the quickest path based on distance but also takes current traffic conditions into account. This feature can be invaluable during rush hours or when unexpected delays occur, as it updates your route in real time to avoid traffic jams and road closures.

For those who prefer public transit, the Maps app offers detailed transit schedules and directions. Whether you're taking the subway, a bus, or a train, the app provides step-by-step navigation, including the location of the nearest transit stop and the departure times of upcoming services. This integration makes it an essential tool for urban commuters who rely on public transportation.

The Maps app also includes a feature called "Flyover" in select cities, which offers a rich, immersive experience by providing high-resolution aerial views of major urban areas. You can virtually navigate through these cities in a stunning, 3D-like interface that shows buildings, landmarks, and other notable features in incredible detail. This feature not only helps with navigation but also enhances your understanding of the city's layout.

For those who love to explore the outdoors, the Maps app provides comprehensive information on hiking trails, parks, and natural landmarks. With details on terrain, difficulty, and scenic highlights, the app can help you plan outdoor adventures that match your skill level and interests.

Moreover, the Maps app ensures that your favorite places are always at your fingertips. You can create a list of favorite locations for quick access, whether they're frequent destinations or wish-list places for future visits. Additionally, you can share your location with friends and family directly from the app, making it easier to coordinate meetups or ensure safety during solo travels.

In essence, the Maps app on your iPhone 14 is much more than a standard GPS navigator; it's a dynamic travel companion that adapts to your needs, whether you're commuting, traveling for pleasure, or exploring the great outdoors. With each update, Apple continues to enhance its functionality, adding features that cater to the diverse needs of modern travelers and making it an indispensable tool in your digital toolkit.

Conclusion to Chapter 3: Exploring Essential Apps

As we wrap up this exploration of the essential apps on your iPhone 14, you now have a deeper understanding of how these tools can enrich your daily digital interactions. From navigating the vast offerings of the App Store to surfing the web with Safari, managing your communications via Mail, and finding your way with Maps, these applications are designed to enhance your productivity and connectivity. They are not merely tools but gateways to expanding your capabilities and efficiency. Continue to explore these apps, customize your experience, and discover new ways to integrate their functionality into your life. Remember, your iPhone 14 is as dynamic as the apps it supports, and mastering these essentials is just the beginning of unlocking its potential.

Chapter 4: Managing Your Contacts and Calendar

In our fast-paced world, managing personal and professional relationships alongside our daily schedules is crucial for staying productive and connected. Your iPhone 14 is equipped with sophisticated tools designed to streamline this aspect of your life. In this chapter, we explore the integrated features of your iPhone that assist in managing your contacts and calendar. We'll start by examining how to add and edit contacts in the Contacts app, ensuring that you can always reach your important connections efficiently. Next, we'll delve into syncing these contacts across all your Apple devices, maintaining consistency and accessibility wherever you go. Following that, we'll navigate through managing your calendar events, making sure you never miss an important date. Lastly, we'll cover how to effectively use reminders and alarms to keep you on track with your daily tasks and appointments, making your iPhone an essential companion in your organized life.

Adding and Editing Contacts

Managing your social and professional circles efficiently begins with how well you manage your contacts. Your iPhone 14 makes this crucial task effortless with its intuitive Contacts app, designed to keep all your important connections just a tap away. This guide will walk you through the process of adding and editing contacts on your iPhone, ensuring that you always have your network organized and accessible.

To begin adding a new contact, open the Contacts app from your home screen. Here, you'll find a plus icon usually located at the top right of the screen. Tapping this icon opens a new contact form, which prompts you to enter details such as name, phone number, email address, and more. The iPhone allows you to add a wealth of information to each contact entry, including but not limited to physical addresses, birthday dates, and even related social media handles. This depth of detail not only helps in keeping your contacts organized but also enhances your interactions by keeping important personal details at your fingertips.

Each field in the new contact form is optional, allowing you to customize the information you store based on your preferences and the nature of your relationship with the person. For instance, you might choose to add a nickname or a company name, helping to contextualize contacts in a way that suits your needs. Additionally, you can assign a specific ringtone or text tone to each contact, which can be particularly helpful for identifying callers without needing to look at your phone.

Editing a contact is just as straightforward. From the Contacts app, simply select the contact you wish to edit. You'll see an 'edit' button, usually at the top right corner of the screen. Tapping this button will allow you to modify any of the contact's details or add additional information as needed. Changes are saved automatically when you tap 'Done', ensuring that your contact list is always up-to-date.

Moreover, the iPhone 14 Contacts app integrates with your social apps, pulling in relevant contact details from various sources like email and social media, consolidating all information into a unified contact card. This feature minimizes duplication and keeps your contacts synchronized across all platforms.

For those who manage business contacts, the ability to add custom labels to phone numbers or email addresses can be invaluable. Whether labeling a contact's number as 'work', 'home', or something more specific, these labels can help you navigate your network efficiently during busy workdays.

In conclusion, the Contacts app on your iPhone 14 is a powerful tool designed to keep your social and professional networks well-organized. With simple additions and edits, coupled with comprehensive integration and customization options, managing your contacts becomes a seamless part of your daily routine, enhancing both your productivity and your connectivity.

Syncing Your Contacts Across Devices

In our interconnected world, having consistent access to your contact list across multiple devices not only enhances convenience but also ensures that you're never without important contact information when you need it. The iPhone 14, leveraging iCloud, offers a seamless solution for syncing your contacts across all your Apple devices, from your iPhone to your iPad and Mac. This integration reflects a fundamental aspect of Apple's ecosystem: continuity.

To begin syncing your contacts, the first step is to ensure that iCloud is set up on your iPhone 14. This involves signing into your iCloud account under Settings and navigating to the iCloud menu. Here, you'll find a list of applications and features that can be synced with iCloud, including contacts. By toggling Contacts to 'On', you enable iCloud to start syncing your contacts across all devices linked to your iCloud account.

Once enabled, any addition, deletion, or modification made to your contacts on one device automatically updates across all your devices. This means if you add a new contact on your iPhone, it will appear on your iPad and Mac without any further action required from you. Similarly, editing a contact's details on your Mac will reflect the changes on your iPhone and any other connected device. This real-time updating eliminates the need for manual transfers or duplicate entries, simplifying contact management significantly.

Beyond the convenience of having your contacts synced, this feature is also a safeguard against data loss. Should you lose your phone or need to replace it, your contacts are safely stored in iCloud and can be restored to any new device during the setup process. Simply log into your iCloud account, and your contacts will populate on the new device, just as they were on the old one.

For those who use multiple Apple IDs, such as one for personal use and another for work, the iPhone allows you to configure which accounts you want to sync contacts from. This can be managed from the Mail, Contacts, Calendars settings, where you can specify which accounts should have contacts enabled and thereby control what appears in your phone's contact list.

It is also worth mentioning the security aspect of iCloud syncing. Apple prioritizes user privacy and data security, employing end-to-end encryption for data synced with iCloud, including your contacts. This means that your contact information is protected from unauthorized access both during transmission and when stored on iCloud servers.

Furthermore, for those who are part of a family sharing group, iCloud provides an option to share contacts among family members easily. This can be particularly useful for sharing contact information of mutual friends, family members, or services without having to manually send the contact details to each person.

In summary, the ability to sync your contacts across devices using iCloud on your iPhone 14 not only streamlines your connectivity but also enriches your user experience. It ensures that your contact list is always current and accessible, no matter which device you are using, and it safeguards your important information, all while maintaining strict privacy standards.

Managing Your Calendar Events

The Calendar app on your iPhone 14 is a versatile tool designed to keep your schedule organized and easily accessible. Whether it's for business meetings, personal appointments, or social events, the Calendar app helps you manage your time efficiently, ensuring you never miss an important date.

Upon opening the Calendar app, you're greeted with a clean, intuitive interface that allows you to view your schedule in different formats: day, week, month, or year. This flexibility lets you have a quick overview or a detailed look at your upcoming events, depending on your needs at the moment. Adding a new event is as simple as tapping on a specific time slot or using the plus icon typically found in the upper right corner of the screen. Here, you can enter essential details about the event, such as title, location, start and end times, and even set up a travel time alert.

One of the standout features of the Calendar app is its integration with other native apps on your iPhone 14. For instance, if you receive an email with a date and time mentioned, the Calendar can automatically suggest adding this as an event. This intelligent feature saves time and enhances productivity by recognizing date and time information across apps, streamlining the process of keeping your calendar up-to-date.

The Calendar app also allows you to set up multiple calendars for different areas of your life, such as work, home, or hobbies. This organization makes it easy to filter your view based on what part of your life you are managing at the moment, and you can toggle these calendars on or off to focus on specific events without distraction. Each calendar can be color-coded, providing a visual cue that helps quickly distinguish between different types of activities at a glance.

For those who work across different time zones, the Calendar app provides support to manage this with ease. It allows you to see the time of the event in both your current location's time zone and the time zone where the event is occurring, which is invaluable for remote workers and global teams.

Sharing your calendar with family, friends, or colleagues is another powerful feature. You can invite others to events you've created, which helps in coordinating group activities or meetings. Invitations can be sent directly from the event creation screen, and recipients can RSVP, providing immediate updates on who will be attending.

Additionally, the Calendar app is not just about scheduling appointments; it's also about getting reminders. You can set up alerts for events, which can be customized to occur minutes, hours, or days before the event, ensuring you're always prepared. The app can also suggest optimal departure times based on traffic conditions, helping you arrive on time.

The iPhone 14's Calendar app is more than a simple scheduling tool—it's an integrated part of your daily management system. It works seamlessly within the Apple ecosystem to enhance your productivity and ensure you're always connected with your commitments. Whether you're planning your day or organizing a large event, the Calendar app provides all the functionalities you need to manage your time effectively.

HOME SCREEN   **CALENDAR**   **NEW EVENT**

CLICK ON
CALENDAR ICON

CLICK ON + ICON

CLICK O
ICON TO
NEW E

Setting Reminders and Alarms

In the bustling rhythm of modern life, staying on top of your tasks and appointments can be a challenge. Fortunately, your iPhone 14 is equipped with intuitive tools like the Reminders and Clock apps, designed to help you manage your time efficiently and ensure you never miss a beat. These tools are not just functional; they are integrated into the daily operations of your iPhone, making them indispensable for keeping track of everything from daily chores to important meetings.

The Reminders app on your iPhone 14 is a versatile tool for organizing your tasks. It allows you to create, edit, and manage reminders with ease. To add a new reminder, simply tap the "New Reminder" button, type in your task, and select a date and time for when you need to be reminded. You can specify as much or as little detail as you like, from assigning a reminder to a specific list to adding a location-based trigger, which notifies you when you arrive at or leave a particular location.

One of the key features of the Reminders app is its ability to integrate with Siri, Apple's voice-activated assistant. You can create a reminder simply by using your voice, such as saying, "Hey Siri, remind me to call John at 2 PM tomorrow." This hands-free functionality is especially useful when you're on the go, allowing you to set reminders without ever having to stop and type.

Reminders can be categorized into lists, helping you organize tasks by theme or project. For example, you might have a list for grocery shopping, another for work-related tasks, and a third for personal goals. This organization makes it easier to see at a glance what tasks you have coming up in different areas of your life, enhancing your overall productivity.

In addition to reminders, your iPhone 14's Clock app provides powerful alarm features that are essential for daily scheduling. Setting an alarm is straightforward: open the Clock app, go to the Alarm tab, and tap the plus sign to create a new alarm. You can customize each alarm, choosing which days of the week it should repeat, the sound it should play, and even the option to set a label that reminds you why the alarm was set.

The Clock app also includes a bedtime feature, which helps you maintain a consistent sleep schedule. By setting your desired sleep and wake times, your iPhone 14 can remind you when it's time to start winding down for the evening, enhancing your overall well-being by encouraging better sleep habits.

Furthermore, both the Reminders and Clock apps are integrated with other iOS features, such as the Notification Center and Apple Watch, ensuring that you're alerted across all your devices, so you never miss out on what's important.

Overall, the combination of the Reminders and Clock apps on your iPhone 14 is designed to offer you a comprehensive suite of tools for time management. Whether it's remembering to pay a bill, waking up on time for an early meeting, or ensuring you're reminded of a friend's birthday, these apps work seamlessly to keep your day running smoothly and keep you punctually informed.

Conclusion to Chapter 4: Managing Your Contacts and Calendar

As we conclude our exploration of the Contacts and Calendar functionalities of your iPhone 14, you now possess a thorough understanding of how to leverage these tools to enhance your daily interactions and scheduling efficiency. From the simplicity of adding and editing contacts to the robustness of managing detailed calendar events, your iPhone serves as your personal assistant, ensuring that you're always connected and informed. The ability to sync your information across devices and set intelligent reminders and alarms further enriches your experience, providing continuity and reliability in your busy life. With these capabilities, your iPhone 14 not only simplifies routine tasks but also empowers you to create a well-organized and smoothly run lifestyle. Continue to explore and utilize these features as you navigate your day-to-day activities, and you will find your iPhone to be an indispensable tool in managing your personal and professional life.

Chapter 5: Mastering Photos and Videos

In the digital age, mastering the art of capturing and refining photos and videos is essential, and your iPhone 14 is equipped to help you excel at both. This chapter dives into the comprehensive features of your iPhone's Camera and Photos apps, turning you from a casual photographer into a skilled creator. We start by exploring the camera's dynamic capabilities for taking stunning photos, followed by techniques for recording videos that are both clear and compelling. We'll also cover how to keep your growing library organized, making it easy to retrieve any photo or video. Finally, we delve into the powerful editing tools available right on your device, which can transform your captures into polished, professional-quality images and videos. Whether you're documenting daily life or crafting visual masterpieces, this chapter will guide you through mastering these essential skills.

Taking Photos with the Camera App

In the realm of smartphone technology, the iPhone 14 stands out with its advanced camera app, designed to make photography an intuitive, accessible, and highly gratifying experience. Whether you're capturing life's everyday moments or special occasions, the iPhone 14's camera app ensures that every shot you take is stunning. This section explores the various features and techniques to maximize the potential of your iPhone's camera, helping you take professional-quality photos with just a few taps.

The camera app on your iPhone 14 is engineered with both amateur photographers and seasoned professionals in mind, making it versatile for all levels of experience. Opening the app presents you with a clean and user-friendly interface, dominated by the shutter button centrally located at the bottom of the screen. This simplicity belies the sophistication hidden just beneath the surface, where a variety of modes can be accessed with a simple swipe.

You'll find several shooting modes available, including Photo, Portrait, and Pano. Each mode is tailored to different photography needs. Photo mode is the standard setting, suitable for most situations. Portrait mode, enhanced by sophisticated algorithms, blurs the background to give a professional depth-of-field effect, emphasizing the subject. Pano mode allows you to capture expansive landscapes by stitching together a sequence of images into a single panoramic photo.

The iPhone 14 camera also includes a Night mode, which automatically activates in low-light settings. This mode is a game-changer for casual photography, significantly enhancing photo quality under challenging lighting conditions. It works by extending the shutter speed, allowing more light to hit the sensor, thereby brightening the photo without compromising on detail.

For those interested in more controlled photography, the Pro settings can be invaluable. By tapping on the arrow icon at the top of the screen in Photo mode, you unlock manual controls such as exposure adjustment, aspect ratio changes, and the option to switch on a grid for better composition alignment. These settings empower you to take charge of the photographic process, adjusting parameters to suit your vision.

Focusing is another critical aspect managed seamlessly by the app. A simple tap on the screen allows you to focus on any subject instantly, and you can easily lock the focus by long-pressing the screen. This feature is particularly useful when composing shots that require a specific focal point to stand out.

Moreover, the iPhone 14 camera supports Live Photos, capturing moments with motion and sound. When enabled, the camera records what happens just before and after you take a picture, bringing your photos to life whenever you press and hold them in your gallery.

In mastering the Camera app on your iPhone 14, you not only harness the capability to capture images that are visually appealing but also engage with technology that makes photography a more dynamic and expressive part of your digital life. Whether you are documenting, creating, or exploring, the camera on your iPhone 14 is an essential tool that promises to enhance how you see and share your world.

Recording Videos

In today's digital era, video recording has become an essential form of expression and communication, capturing everything from everyday moments to once-in-a-lifetime events. The iPhone 14 elevates this experience with its advanced video capabilities, allowing anyone to produce high-quality footage with ease. This section delves into how to maximize the potential of your iPhone's video recording features, ensuring that you can capture, create, and share your visual stories with clarity and impact.

The video recording function on your iPhone 14 is seamlessly integrated into the Camera app, making it incredibly accessible. Switching from photo to video mode is as simple as swiping right on the camera mode selector, which is conveniently located just above the shutter button. Once in video mode, you will notice that the interface slightly adjusts to accommodate video-specific settings, including a prominent red record button.

One of the standout features of the iPhone 14's video capability is its ability to record in different resolutions and frame rates. You can choose from 4K at 24, 30, or 60 frames per second (fps) to 1080p HD at 30 or 60 fps, depending on your needs. Higher frame rates are perfect for capturing fast action and can be used to create smooth slow-motion effects in post-production, while higher resolutions ensure that your video remains crisp and detailed, even when viewed on large screens.

To start recording, simply tap the red record button. While recording, you can also take advantage of the iPhone's autofocus and exposure features, which adjust in real-time to keep your video sharp and well-lit. If you need more control over these aspects, a long press on the screen lets you lock both focus and exposure, giving you consistent visual output throughout your recording session.

The iPhone 14 also supports advanced video formats like HDR and Dolby Vision, which bring incredible depth and realism to your videos. These technologies enhance the color and brightness of your recordings, making them vibrant and true to life. This is particularly beneficial when capturing videos in varied lighting conditions, ensuring that your footage retains quality and detail.

Audio recording is another critical component of video production, and the iPhone 14 doesn't disappoint. It features multiple microphones that capture stereo sound, enhancing the audio fidelity of your videos. This multi-microphone setup not only records sound with clarity but also helps in reducing background noise, focusing on the audio in front of the camera.

For those who love to create more dynamic and cinematic videos, the iPhone 14 offers features like time-lapse and slow-motion. These can be selected directly in the camera interface and provide you with creative ways to capture and present time and motion in your videos, adding a layer of artistic expression to your recordings.

In essence, the video recording capabilities of the iPhone 14 are designed to empower creators of all levels. Whether you're documenting a family gathering, producing content for social media, or creating a short film, the iPhone 14's Camera app provides you with a suite of professional-quality tools that make it possible to bring your vision to life effortlessly.

HOME SCREEN

TAP AND HOLD
CAMERA ICON

PHOTOS

CLICK HERE TO
TAKE PICTURES

VIDEOS

TAP ON VIDEO TO
SWITCH

CLICK HERE TO
RECORD VIDEOS

Organizing Your Photos and Videos

In the age of digital photography and videography, managing the ever-growing library of media on your iPhone 14 can seem daunting. However, Apple's Photos app provides robust tools designed to help you organize and access your photos and videos quickly and efficiently, turning potential chaos into a well-ordered collection that enhances your enjoyment and utility of your media.

The Photos app on the iPhone 14 automatically sorts your images and videos into a variety of categories, making navigation straightforward. Upon opening the app, you'll find your media organized by Years, Months, Days, and All Photos, which allows you to view your content according to different time frames. This temporal sorting helps you scroll through life's moments in a chronological storyline, making it easy to relive memories from specific periods.

Another powerful feature of the Photos app is the 'Albums' tab. Here, you can create custom albums to categorize your photos and videos according to themes, events, or any other criteria you choose. Creating an album is as simple as selecting the 'plus' icon, naming the album, and then adding the relevant media. For instance, you might have an album for family vacations, another for everyday snapshots, and a third for professional photography work. Albums not only help in segregating photos for easy access but also in sharing collections with others.

The Photos app also utilizes advanced AI technology to categorize images by recognizing faces, places, and even objects within your photos. The 'People' album automatically groups photos by the faces identified, so pictures of the same person are filed together. Similarly, the 'Places' album uses geotagging data to sort images based on where they were taken, displaying your photos on a map so you can easily see all the places you've captured.

Search functionality within the Photos app is exceptionally robust, enabling you to find images based on a wide array of criteria. You can search for locations, dates, people's names, or even objects and scenes like "beaches" or "birthdays." This deep level of indexing allows for quick retrieval of photos without the need to manually browse through your entire library.

For those who capture a lot of video, the Photos app distinguishes between stills and moving pictures by organizing videos into their own dedicated album automatically. This separation allows for easier management of videos, especially when editing or sharing them.

Moreover, the Photos app integrates seamlessly with iCloud, ensuring that all your photos and videos are backed up and accessible on any Apple device. When you make organizational changes on one device, like creating an album or tagging a favorite, these changes are synchronized across all devices connected to your iCloud account. This feature not only secures your precious memories against loss but also keeps your photo and video organization consistent no matter which device you're using.

In summary, the Photos app on your iPhone 14 is a comprehensive tool for managing your photographic and video content. With its advanced organizational features, AI-powered sorting, and seamless iCloud integration, it transforms what could be an overwhelming collection of images and videos into an easily navigable, enjoyable library, enhancing your multimedia experience significantly.

Editing Your Photos and Videos

The ability to capture high-quality photos and videos on your iPhone 14 is just the beginning. With the integrated Photos app, you also have a powerful suite of editing tools at your fingertips, allowing you to enhance, modify, and transform your media into polished, creative works of art. This section will explore the various features of the Photos app that make editing both accessible and deeply functional for photographers and videographers at any skill level.

Upon selecting a photo or video to edit in the Photos app, you are presented with a streamlined interface that offers a range of adjustments, filters, and cropping tools. For photos, editing begins with simple adjustments such as light and color. Sliders for exposure, brightness, contrast, and saturation let you refine your photos to better reflect the mood or enhance the details. The brilliance and highlights can be tweaked to make your photos pop, while shadows and black point adjustments can add depth and drama to your images.

Beyond basic adjustments, the Photos app includes a set of filters that can quickly change the look and feel of your photographs. From dramatic noir effects to subtle vintage fades, filters offer a one-tap solution to creatively alter your images. Each filter can be applied with varying intensity, giving you control over the strength of the effect.

For more detailed refinements, the Photos app provides options like selective color adjustments and white balance settings. These tools allow you to focus on specific colors in your image, enhancing or toning down hues without affecting the overall color balance. Similarly, white balance adjustments can help correct color casts that occur in different lighting conditions, ensuring that whites are true to life and that the overall coloration is balanced.

Editing videos in the Photos app offers a similarly intuitive experience. You can trim videos to your desired length by dragging the edges of the timeline, or adjust the exposure and color settings to enhance the video's visual appeal. Other video-specific editing features include the ability to auto-enhance the quality, adjust the frame rate, or even mute the audio directly within the app.

The Photos app also supports advanced editing features like portrait editing on photos taken in Portrait mode. This feature allows you to adjust the depth of field effect after the photo has been taken, blurring the background to different degrees to make your subject stand out more or less prominently. Additionally, you can apply lighting effects to portrait photos, simulating studio-quality light scenarios that enhance the facial features of your subjects.

Once your editing is complete, saving your changes is straightforward, with the option to overwrite the original file or save a copy as a new file. This flexibility ensures that you can always go back to the original media if needed.

In summary, the editing tools provided in the iPhone 14's Photos app are designed not just for cosmetic adjustments but to give users creative control over their media. Whether you're making slight tweaks to photos or conducting major edits on videos, these tools empower you to achieve professional-level results directly from your phone, transforming your captured moments into compelling stories and visuals.

Conclusion to Chapter 5: Mastering Photos and Videos

Having explored the powerful capabilities of your iPhone 14 for capturing and enhancing photos and videos, you are now equipped to take full advantage of these innovative tools. From the basics of taking sharp and well-composed pictures to the intricacies of video recording and the artful editing of both, your iPhone is an indispensable tool for digital storytelling. As you continue to use these features, your skills will refine, and your ability to express yourself visually will expand. The organizational strategies and editing techniques discussed will help keep your digital memories not only safe but also ready to be shared and enjoyed. Continue to explore, experiment, and push the boundaries of what you can create with your iPhone 14, making each photo and video not just a moment captured, but a story told.

Chapter 6: Entertainment on Your iPhone 14

In today's digital era, your iPhone 14 is not merely a communication device but a comprehensive entertainment hub. This chapter explores the myriad ways in which the iPhone 14 caters to your entertainment needs, transforming every interaction into an enjoyable experience. Whether it's immersing yourself in music with Apple Music, catching up on your favorite movies and TV shows, diving into the vast world of digital reading, or escaping into engaging video games, your iPhone 14 has something to offer for every type of entertainment enthusiast. Each section of this chapter will guide you through these entertainment options, showcasing how to maximize the enjoyment of your device's features. Prepare to unlock the full potential of your iPhone as your ultimate portable entertainment system, ensuring that wherever you are, your entertainment is just a tap away.

Exploring Apple Music

Apple Music on your iPhone 14 is much more than a streaming service; it's a comprehensive platform for music discovery, enjoyment, and integration into your daily life. Whether you're an audiophile, a casual listener, or someone looking to find the perfect soundtrack for different moments, Apple Music provides an array of features that make listening to music an enriching and effortless experience.

Upon launching Apple Music, you're greeted by a vibrant and user-friendly interface that invites exploration. The service offers over 70 million songs, curated playlists, and live radio stations. One of the standout features of Apple Music is its personalized recommendations. The service uses sophisticated algorithms that learn from your listening habits to suggest new songs and artists you might like, effectively tailoring your listening experience to fit your personal tastes.

Navigation within the app is intuitive. The bottom of the screen hosts tabs such as 'Library,' 'For You,' 'Browse,' and 'Radio,' each offering distinct ways to interact with your music. 'Library' keeps all your saved and downloaded music organized, allowing quick access to your favorites whenever you want. The 'For You' section presents a mix of albums, singles, and playlists recommended based on your previous listening activities, making it an excellent tool for discovering new music that fits your style.

In the 'Browse' tab, Apple Music opens up the world of new releases, top charts, and genres, providing a global perspective on what's trending. This section not only keeps you up-to-date with the latest hits but also exposes you to a wide range of genres from around the world, broadening your musical horizons.

For those who enjoy radio, Apple Music's 'Radio' tab features several options, including Beats 1, which broadcasts live to over 100 countries. Beats 1 offers interviews, music premieres, and diverse shows by major artists and DJs. This integration of traditional radio with modern streaming capabilities creates a unique platform where users can connect with the music world live and in real time.

Another significant aspect of Apple Music is its seamless integration with Siri, Apple's intelligent assistant. This feature allows you to control music playback with voice commands, a convenient option especially when you're driving or your iPhone is out of reach. You can ask Siri to play specific tracks, albums, or even query by lyrics when you can't remember the name of a song.

Furthermore, Apple Music offers a social feature called 'Connect,' which allows artists to share behind-the-scenes photos, lyrics, and other exclusive content with their fans. This feature not only keeps you close to your favorite artists but also enriches your understanding of their creative processes.

Apple Music on the iPhone 14 does more than play music; it provides a dynamic and immersive musical experience that adapits to your personal preferences and lifestyle. Whether you're looking to keep up with the latest tracks, explore new genres, or just enjoy your favorite songs, Apple Music is equipped to deliver a stellar auditory experience anytime, anywhere.

Watching Movies and TV Shows

The iPhone 14 transforms into a portable cinema, offering a high-quality viewing experience that allows you to enjoy movies and TV shows wherever you go. With its Retina display providing vivid colors and sharp resolution, coupled with spatial audio for immersive sound, watching media on your iPhone is both a convenience and a delight. This section explores how your iPhone 14 serves as a gateway to a world of cinematic and television content through various apps and features designed to cater to your viewing preferences.

One of the primary portals for watching movies and TV shows on your iPhone 14 is the Apple TV app. This app consolidates content from your iTunes library and subscriptions, making it easy to find what you want to watch. The Apple TV app not only allows you to rent or buy movies and TV shows but also offers recommendations based on your viewing habits. It features a user-friendly interface where shows and movies are neatly categorized under headings like "Watch Now," "Up Next," which keeps track of what you're currently watching, and "Discover," which suggests new content you might enjoy.

For subscribers to Apple TV+, Apple's own streaming service, the app offers an array of original programming, featuring everything from dramas and comedies to documentaries and children's programming. These Apple Originals are available in 4K HDR and Dolby Atmos sound, ensuring that your viewing experience is as close to theater-quality as possible.

Moreover, the integration with other streaming services through the Apple TV app, such as Hulu, Amazon Prime Video, and Disney+, means that you have access to a vast library of additional content all in one place. This integration helps streamline your viewing process, allowing you to spend less time searching and more time enjoying your favorite shows and movies.

Accessibility features in the Apple TV app also enhance the viewing experience for all users. Subtitles and closed captions are available for the hearing impaired, and "Audio Descriptions" describe what is happening on screen for the visually impaired. These features ensure that entertainment on the iPhone 14 is inclusive, allowing everyone to enjoy the vast world of digital media.

Additionally, the iPhone 14 is perfect for those on the move, thanks to its ability to download content directly to your device. Whether you're commuting, traveling, or simply need to save data, you can download your chosen episodes or films to watch offline. This feature ensures that your entertainment is not interrupted by connectivity issues, providing continuous, high-quality playback.

In conclusion, watching movies and TV shows on the iPhone 14 offers more than just streaming; it's a comprehensive entertainment experience that adapts to your lifestyle. With easy access to a wide range of content, superior video and audio capabilities, and thoughtful integration of accessibility features, your iPhone 14 is your ticket to endless hours of entertainment, tailored just for you.

Reading Books and Magazines

The iPhone 14 isn't just a tool for communication or multimedia entertainment; it also serves as a portable library where you can immerse yourself in the world of books and magazines anytime, anywhere. Thanks to a variety of apps and features tailored for readers, your iPhone transforms into an e-reader that offers convenience, accessibility, and a vast selection of reading materials. This chapter delves into how you can utilize your iPhone 14 to engage with literature and periodicals in digital form, enhancing your reading experience.

The primary gateway to reading on your iPhone 14 is through Apple Books, an app that provides access to a massive collection of books and audiobooks across various genres. Upon opening Apple Books, you're greeted by a user-friendly interface that allows you to browse and purchase new books, download them for offline reading, and organize your personal library with ease. The app also offers personalized recommendations based on your reading habits, helping you discover your next great read without extensive searching.

For magazine lovers, Apple News+ is an invaluable resource available on your iPhone 14. It offers access to hundreds of magazines and leading newspapers, all within a single app. The visual layout of Apple News+ is designed to enhance the reading experience on a mobile device, with richly illustrated articles and interactive features that make the most of the iPhone's touch interface. Subscribing to Apple News+ not only gives you comprehensive access to current and past issues but also ensures that you stay informed with high-quality journalism from around the world.

One of the standout features for readers is the convenience of synchronization. Purchases made through Apple Books are available across all your Apple devices, allowing you to start reading on your iPhone and pick up where you left off on your iPad or Mac. This seamless syncing extends to bookmarks, notes, and highlights, making it easy to transition between devices without losing your place or your thoughts.

For those who enjoy listening to stories, the Audiobooks section within Apple Books offers a wide range of titles, from bestsellers to classics. The ability to listen to audiobooks is perfect for multitasking or enjoying literature on the go, whether you're commuting, exercising, or simply relaxing at home. The audio playback controls are optimized for ease of use, including features such as sleep timers and speed adjustments, enhancing the audiobook listening experience.

The reading experience on the iPhone 14 is also tailored for accessibility. Features such as adjustable text sizes, font styles, and background colors allow you to customize your reading interface to suit your visual preferences. For those with specific accessibility needs, the iPhone includes options like VoiceOver, which reads content aloud, and Speak Screen, which can recite the text from books, articles, and emails.

In essence, the iPhone 14 offers a rich and accessible reading environment that caters to book lovers and magazine aficionados alike. With powerful apps like Apple Books and Apple News+, your mobile device becomes a hub of literary exploration and enjoyment, ensuring that your favorite books and magazines are never more than a few taps away. Whether you're deepening your knowledge, escaping into a novel, or staying updated with current events, your iPhone 14 enriches your reading experiences in countless ways.

Playing Games on Your iPhone 14

The iPhone 14 is not just a tool for productivity and communication—it's also a powerful gaming console that fits in your pocket. With cutting-edge hardware, a vast ecosystem of games via the App Store, and enhanced features like Apple Arcade, your iPhone 14 is equipped to provide a premium gaming experience. Whether you're a casual gamer or a dedicated enthusiast, the iPhone's capabilities ensure that you have access to a diverse array of games, offering everything from quick puzzles to immersive adventures.

When you launch the App Store, the "Games" section presents you with curated lists of games, trending titles, and new releases. The variety is expansive, catering to all tastes and preferences. Games on the iPhone 14 are more than mere pastimes; they are gateways into vivid worlds thanks to the powerful A-series processor and advanced graphics. The smooth performance and fast loading times mean that games not only look spectacular on the Retina display but also run seamlessly, providing an engaging user experience without frustrating lags or interruptions.

One of the standout features for gaming on the iPhone 14 is Apple Arcade. This subscription service offers access to a library of premium games, free of ads and in-app purchases. Apple Arcade games range from award-winning indie titles to exclusive releases from renowned creators. The service is designed to offer a high-quality gaming experience with the convenience of a single subscription. With Apple Arcade, users can explore a variety of games, all optimized to take full advantage of the iPhone's hardware capabilities, ensuring the best possible performance.

Gaming on the iPhone 14 is also a social experience. Many games support multiplayer options, allowing you to connect with friends or gamers around the world. Whether it's competing in real-time strategy games, collaborating in adventure quests, or challenging friends in puzzle games, the social element adds a rich layer of enjoyment and competition to the gaming experience.

Moreover, the integration of gaming with other Apple services enhances your interactive sessions. For instance, game progress can be saved via iCloud, allowing you to pick up where you left off on any Apple device. This feature is particularly useful for those who play on multiple devices, such as starting a game on an iPhone and continuing on an iPad.

The iPhone 14's gaming experience is also tailored for convenience. Notifications can be managed to ensure that you aren't disturbed during gaming sessions, and settings are available to optimize battery usage, which can be crucial during extended play. Additionally, the Health app can track the time spent playing games, helping you maintain a balanced digital lifestyle.

In essence, playing games on your iPhone 14 offers an immersive and versatile gaming experience. With access to a vast array of titles through the App Store and Apple Arcade, along with powerful performance and convenient features, your iPhone is a premier gaming device. It invites not just interaction but complete engagement with content that excites, challenges, and entertains, making every gaming session uniquely satisfying.

Conclusion to Chapter 6: Entertainment on Your iPhone 14

As we conclude our exploration of the entertainment capabilities of the iPhone 14, it's clear that this device is a powerhouse for personal amusement and digital engagement. Through Apple Music, the Apple TV app, Apple Books, and a plethora of gaming options, the iPhone 14 ensures that your entertainment preferences are not only met but exceeded. Each feature is designed to integrate seamlessly into your lifestyle, providing on-demand entertainment suited to your tastes and preferences. As you continue to explore these features, you'll find that your iPhone 14 can redefine your leisure moments, making every experience richer and more accessible. Whether you're at home or on the go, your iPhone is ready to entertain, educate, and enchant. So, dive into the vast array of options available at your fingertips, and make the most of your iPhone 14 as your all-in-one entertainment device.

Chapter 7: Staying Safe and Secure

In an era where digital security is more crucial than ever, your iPhone 14 is designed to provide robust protection against a wide range of security threats. This chapter delves into the essential practices and features that help safeguard your personal information and enhance your device's security. From setting up biometric security measures such as Touch ID or Face ID to creating strong, unbreakable passwords, we cover all the bases. Additionally, we'll guide you through best practices for protecting your privacy and arming yourself against common threats like scams and phishing attempts. Each section is tailored to equip you with the knowledge and tools needed to secure your digital life effectively. By understanding and implementing these security measures, you can enjoy the full potential of your iPhone 14 with peace of mind, knowing that your data is safe and secure.

Setting up Touch ID or Face ID

In the digital age, securing your personal information is crucial, and the iPhone 14 makes it simple and efficient with advanced biometric security features like Touch ID and Face ID. These technologies not only protect your device but also provide a seamless and quick way to access your phone without compromising security. This section guides you through setting up these features, highlighting their benefits and the layers of security they add to your iPhone 14.

Touch ID is Apple's fingerprint recognition feature that makes use of a small sensor embedded in the Home button (on models that have one) or the power button (on newer models without a Home button). Setting up Touch ID involves placing your finger on the button so that the sensor can capture and record your fingerprint from multiple angles. The process requires you to lift and rest your finger slightly differently several times, ensuring that the iPhone captures a comprehensive map of your fingerprint. The setup can be found in the Settings app under 'Touch ID & Passcode.' Here, you can also designate what Touch ID will be used for—unlocking your iPhone, confirming downloads, and authorizing Apple Pay transactions. The process is intuitive and only takes a few minutes, but it significantly enhances your device's security by ensuring that only your fingerprints can unlock your phone.

Face ID, introduced with the iPhone X, uses a sophisticated facial recognition system that projects and analyzes over 30,000 invisible dots to create a precise depth map of your face. This technology adapts to changes in your appearance, such as wearing cosmetics, growing facial hair, or wearing glasses. To set up Face ID, you'll go to 'Face ID & Passcode' in your Settings app, where you'll be prompted to position your face in front of your iPhone and slowly complete two scans of your face. Face ID is designed to work with hats, scarves, glasses, contact lenses, and many sunglasses, making it versatile for everyday use. Moreover, it's capable of recognizing your face even in the dark, using infrared technology.

Both Touch ID and Face ID are built with your privacy in mind. The data used for either technology is encrypted and protected by the Secure Enclave on your device—it's never stored on Apple servers or backed up to iCloud. This localized storage ensures that your biometric data is kept secure from external threats. Furthermore, these technologies offer a quick and user-friendly way to access secure apps and features on your device. For example, you can use Face ID or Touch ID to securely log in to banking apps, private notes, or confidential documents.

In summary, setting up Touch ID or Face ID on your iPhone 14 provides robust security that guards your device against unauthorized access while offering a seamless and fast way to unlock your phone. Whether you choose the tactile security of Touch ID or the advanced recognition capabilities of Face ID, both technologies give you peace of mind knowing that your personal information and device are well protected.

HOME SCREEN **SETTINGS** **FACE ID**

CLICK ON
SETTINGS
ICON

CLICK ON
FACE ID & PASSCODE

SET UP FACE ID

Creating Strong Passwords

In our interconnected digital world, the strength of your passwords is often the first line of defense against unauthorized access to your personal and financial information. The iPhone 14 provides a suite of features designed to help you create, manage, and maintain strong passwords easily and effectively. This guidance not only enhances your security but also simplifies the process of managing your credentials across various apps and websites.

A strong password is complex, unique, and difficult for others to guess. It should include a mix of uppercase and lowercase letters, numbers, and special characters. The length of the password also plays a critical role in its strength, with longer passwords generally being more secure. On your iPhone 14, the Safari browser and other apps linked to iCloud Keychain can suggest strong, unique passwords for you whenever you create a new account or update an existing one. These suggested passwords are automatically stored in your iCloud Keychain, making them accessible across all your Apple devices yet securely encrypted.

To access and manage your saved passwords, navigate to the Settings app, then to 'Passwords & Accounts,' and finally to 'Website & App Passwords.' Here, you can view all your saved passwords, which are protected and only accessible after you authenticate via Face ID, Touch ID, or your device passcode. This layer of security ensures that even if someone gains access to your iPhone, they cannot access your passwords without additional verification.

Apple also provides a built-in security audit feature for passwords stored in iCloud Keychain. This tool checks your saved passwords against known security breaches and alerts you if a password needs to be changed due to potential exposure. It also identifies weak, easily guessable, or reused passwords and suggests replacing them with stronger ones. By following these recommendations, you can ensure that your passwords are robust and secure.

Furthermore, enabling two-factor authentication (2FA) on your accounts adds an extra layer of security. This process requires not only something you know (your password) but also something you have (such as a code sent to your iPhone) to gain access to your accounts. Many apps and services offer 2FA, and your iPhone can store and autofill these codes for you, making the process both secure and convenient.

Apple's iOS also integrates with third-party password managers through the AutoFill feature. If you prefer to use a different password management tool, you can configure your iPhone to autofill login credentials from these apps just as seamlessly as it does from iCloud Keychain. This flexibility allows you to choose the tool that best fits your needs while still benefiting from the integration and security provided by iOS.

In conclusion, creating and managing strong passwords on your iPhone 14 is a critical component of maintaining your digital security. By leveraging the features offered by iOS, such as password suggestions, iCloud Keychain, and AutoFill, along with the best practices for password creation, you can protect your personal information against unauthorized access and ensure your digital life is both safe and secure.

Protecting Your Privacy

In today's digital age, protecting your privacy is more crucial than ever, especially with the vast amount of personal information stored on devices like your iPhone 14. Apple has long championed privacy as a fundamental right, and the iPhone 14 is equipped with numerous features designed to safeguard your personal data from unauthorized access and ensure you have control over what you share and with whom.

Privacy Settings and Permissions

One of the first steps in protecting your privacy on your iPhone 14 involves customizing your privacy settings. Apple provides a comprehensive privacy menu in the settings app, where you can control which apps have access to your location, contacts, calendars, photos, and more. Each app must request permission before accessing personal data, and you can review and adjust these permissions at any time. This granular control not only enhances security but also builds trust in the apps you use daily.

Location Services

Location services can be particularly sensitive because they track where you are or have been. On the iPhone 14, you can fine-tune location settings to allow apps to access your location always, only while in use, or never. Additionally, iOS provides reports that show which apps have accessed your location information, ensuring transparency. For enhanced privacy, you can use the "While Using the App" permission to limit background tracking, or turn off location services altogether for specific apps.

App Tracking Transparency

With iOS 14 and later, Apple introduced App Tracking Transparency, which requires apps to get your permission before tracking your activities across other companies' apps and websites for advertising or data brokers. This feature gives you the power to prevent apps from selling your data to third parties, a significant step in protecting your personal information from being exploited commercially.

Data Encryption

Encryption is another cornerstone of Apple's privacy protection. Your iPhone 14 encrypts all your data by default, which means it is protected with advanced encryption algorithms that prevent potential intruders from accessing your data without the correct authentication (such as your passcode, Touch ID, or Face ID). This encryption extends to iMessage and FaceTime, where end-to-end encryption ensures that only you and the person you're communicating with can access the contents of your conversations.

Managing Web Browsing Privacy

When browsing the web, Safari offers several privacy-protecting features, such as Intelligent Tracking Prevention, which limits how advertisers and websites track your browsing behavior. Safari also provides privacy reports that show which trackers have been blocked. Additionally, Private Browsing mode can be used to prevent Safari from remembering the pages you visit, your search history, or your AutoFill information.

Secure Wi-Fi and Network Connections

The iPhone 14 also protects your privacy when connected to Wi-Fi networks. It uses a unique, private Wi-Fi address for each network you join to reduce tracking across Wi-Fi networks. Furthermore, iOS regularly updates its security settings and patches to combat new threats, so keeping your device updated is vital for maintaining optimal protection.

In essence, protecting your privacy on your iPhone 14 involves a combination of utilizing built-in security features, being mindful of app permissions, and staying informed about how your data is handled. By taking proactive steps to secure your personal information, you ensure your digital autonomy and safeguard your personal life from being compromised.

Avoiding Scams and Phishing

In an increasingly connected world, the threat of scams and phishing attempts is ever-present. These deceptive practices are designed to trick you into giving away personal information, such as passwords, credit card details, and other sensitive data. Your iPhone 14 comes equipped with several tools and features that help safeguard your information against these threats. Understanding how to recognize and avoid scams and phishing attempts is crucial for maintaining your security and privacy.

Recognizing Phishing Attempts

Phishing often involves fraudsters impersonating legitimate companies or contacts. These attempts can come through various channels, including email, text messages, phone calls, or even through websites and social media. Common signs of phishing include unsolicited requests for personal information, high-pressure tactics, too-good-to-be-true offers, and messages containing poor spelling and grammar. Your iPhone can help identify potentially harmful content, such as marking unknown callers and filtering messages from unknown senders into a separate list.

Email and Message Protection

The Mail app on the iPhone 14 has built-in features to detect and warn you about suspicious emails that may be phishing attempts. If an email comes from an unverified sender or contains links to known phishing sites, Mail will display a warning, advising you to proceed with caution. Similarly, the Messages app filters messages from unknown senders and can alert you to potential spam or phishing content. These features work in the background to provide a layer of protection without disrupting your regular communications.

Safari Security Tools

When browsing online, Safari on your iPhone 14 offers several security features to protect against phishing and scams. Fraudulent website warnings alert you when you're about to visit a suspected phishing site. Safari also prevents suspicious sites from loading and advises you to close the page. Additionally, Safari's privacy report feature allows you to see which trackers have been blocked, giving you greater visibility into who is trying to track your online activities.

Secure Connections and App Security

The App Store provides a secure platform where every app is reviewed by Apple before it's available to download. This review process helps protect against apps that may attempt to scam users. Furthermore, Apple Pay offers a secure way to make payments without directly exposing your credit card number or banking information, reducing the risk of financial scams.

Education and Vigilance

Staying informed about the latest scam tactics and knowing how to respond are your best defenses. Apple provides resources and support that can help you understand security risks and how to avoid them. Regularly updating your iPhone's operating system is also crucial, as each update includes the latest security enhancements to protect against new threats.

By using the built-in features of your iPhone 14 and practicing vigilant security habits, you can significantly reduce your risk of falling victim to scams and phishing. Awareness, combined with the powerful security tools provided by your iPhone, allows you to navigate the digital world with confidence, keeping your personal information safe from fraudsters.

Conclusion to Chapter 7: Staying Safe and Secure

As we conclude our exploration of the security features of the iPhone 14, it's clear that maintaining the safety of your personal information requires diligence and the effective use of the tools at your disposal. This chapter has outlined crucial strategies for protecting your device from unauthorized access and safeguarding your personal data from cyber threats. By setting up Touch ID or Face ID, creating strong passwords, managing privacy settings, and staying vigilant against scams and phishing, you can significantly enhance your security posture. Remember, the responsibility of securing your device not only lies in utilizing these features but also in staying informed about potential threats and adapting to new security practices as they evolve. With the iPhone 14, you have access to industry-leading technology designed to protect your information, giving you confidence and security in your daily digital interactions.

Chapter 8: Accessibility Features

Accessibility is at the heart of Apple's innovation, and the iPhone 14 continues this commitment by offering a wide array of features designed to accommodate users with diverse abilities. This chapter explores the extensive accessibility settings available on your iPhone 14, each meticulously designed to support various needs, from visual and hearing impairments to physical and motor skills challenges. We delve into how you can utilize tools like VoiceOver for audio guidance, Magnifier and Display Zoom for visual aid, and customizable settings that enhance the device's usability. Whether you are looking to tailor your iPhone for specific accessibility requirements or simply wish to explore how these features can make your device more user-friendly, this chapter provides detailed guidance on adjusting your iPhone to better suit your individual needs, ensuring that technology is accessible to everyone.

Exploring Accessibility Settings

The iPhone 14 is designed with inclusivity in mind, offering a range of accessibility features that ensure everyone can use the device effectively, regardless of their physical or sensory abilities. These features are part of Apple's commitment to accessibility, which is integrated deeply into the operating system to provide customized support for all users. This section delves into the various accessibility settings available on your iPhone 14, illustrating how you can tailor the device to meet specific needs and enhance usability.

Accessibility settings on the iPhone 14 are centralized in a dedicated menu within the Settings app. To explore these options, you simply navigate to Settings, then tap on Accessibility. This area is thoughtfully organized into several categories, making it easy to find and activate the features that best suit your requirements.

Vision Accommodations

For users with visual impairments, the iPhone 14 includes several adjustments to enhance screen visibility and interaction. Options like Display & Text Size allow for increasing text size, bolding text for better legibility, and adjusting the display contrast to reduce eye strain. Color Filters can be applied to assist those with color blindness by altering color palettes to improve screen differentiation. Further, the Reduce Motion setting minimizes animation effects to prevent motion triggers and facilitate easier navigation across the user interface.

Hearing Features

Accessibility features for hearing include the Made for iPhone hearing aids support, which syncs with compatible hearing devices to deliver clear audio directly to the user's ears. Visual and vibrating alerts can be set up to replace traditional sound alerts, ensuring that users with hearing loss are aware of incoming notifications or calls. Live Listen, another innovative feature, turns the iPhone into a directional microphone, sending captured audio to Made for iPhone hearing aids, enhancing the ability to hear in noisy environments.

Physical and Motor Skills Adjustments

The iPhone 14 also caters to users with limited physical mobility. Touch Accommodations modify how the screen responds to touch, allowing for customization of tap recognition based on touch duration, movement, and response timing. AssistiveTouch helps users perform gestures like a pinch or multi-finger swipe with a single touch, and can customize taps for easier device control. Additionally, users can opt for Voice Control, which enables complete voice-based navigation to use the device hands-free.

General Accessibility Shortcuts

For convenience, the Accessibility Shortcut—a triple-click of the side or Home button—provides quick access to frequently used accessibility features like VoiceOver, Color Filters, or Magnifier. This shortcut can be customized within the Accessibility menu to toggle specific aids on or off, simplifying their use without navigating through menus.

Understanding and configuring these accessibility settings allows users to fully personalize their iPhone 14 experience. Each feature is designed not just to compensate for a variety of impairments but to empower all users to make the most of their device in the most efficient way possible. By enabling the right settings, the iPhone 14 can become an essential tool for inclusion, providing independence and enhancing the user experience for individuals with diverse accessibility needs.

Using VoiceOver for Audio Guidance

VoiceOver is an advanced screen-reading tool integrated into the iPhone 14, designed to assist users who have visual impairments by speaking the content of the screen aloud. This feature supports a broad range of gestures and commands to interact with applications, making your iPhone accessible on a profound level. Here, we delve into how to activate and utilize VoiceOver, enhancing the usability of your iPhone for those needing auditory feedback to navigate their device.

Activating VoiceOver

To start using VoiceOver on your iPhone 14, you can activate it in one of two ways: through the Settings app or by using Siri. To enable it via Settings, navigate to Settings > Accessibility > VoiceOver, and toggle the switch to turn it on. Alternatively, you can ask Siri to "Turn on VoiceOver" to activate the feature without navigating through menus.

Navigating with VoiceOver

Once enabled, VoiceOver changes the way you interact with your iPhone. Instead of the usual taps, you will use unique gestures designed to work with the audio feedback provided. For example, tapping once on an item selects it, a double-tap activates the selected item, and swiping three fingers will scroll through pages or lists. VoiceOver announces everything you touch, select, and activate, providing continuous audio guidance as you use your phone.

Customizing VoiceOver

VoiceOver is highly customizable to fit individual needs and preferences. Within the VoiceOver settings, you can adjust the speaking rate and pitch to make the voice easier to understand. You can choose from a range of voices in different languages, ensuring the user can select a voice that is most clear and pleasant for them. Additionally, VoiceOver includes a Braille keyboard for direct Braille entry, and support for many Bluetooth-enabled refreshable Braille displays that provide tactile access to output.

Using Rotor for Quick Settings

One of the innovative features within VoiceOver is the "Rotor." By turning two fingers on your iPhone's screen as if you were turning a dial, you can access a customizable list of commands and settings. These can include speaking rate, volume, punctuation levels, and more, allowing for quick adjustments without leaving the VoiceOver environment. This feature is particularly useful for adapting VoiceOver to different contexts, such as reading long articles versus navigating app interfaces.

VoiceOver with Third-Party Apps

Most apps on the App Store are compatible with VoiceOver, as Apple requires all apps to support accessibility features. VoiceOver can read text within the app, describe images if they have been properly labeled, and provide auditory feedback for actions and changes on the screen. This ensures that visually impaired users can enjoy a broad range of applications, from productivity tools to games and educational apps.

Educational and Support Resources

Apple provides extensive resources to help users master VoiceOver, including a detailed user guide available in the Accessibility section of Apple's website. Additionally, many communities and online forums are dedicated to sharing tips and advice on using VoiceOver, helping new users to adapt quickly to this powerful tool.

VoiceOver is more than just a feature; it's a comprehensive solution for visually impaired users to interact with their iPhones confidently and effectively. By mastering VoiceOver, users can enjoy the full functionality of their iPhone 14, ensuring no feature is out of reach due to visual limitations.

Enabling Magnifier and Display Zoom

The iPhone 14 is equipped with accessibility features that cater to users with varying visual needs. Among these features, the Magnifier and Display Zoom stand out for their utility in enhancing visual clarity and detail, making content easier to see and interact with. These tools are especially beneficial for users with low vision, allowing them to use their iPhone more effectively and comfortably.

Magnifier: Turning Your iPhone into a Digital Magnifying Glass

The Magnifier function on the iPhone 14 works like a digital magnifying glass. It uses the iPhone's camera to enlarge objects so you can see them more clearly. This feature is invaluable for reading small text on everything from restaurant menus to labels on medicine bottles. To enable the Magnifier, go to Settings > Accessibility > Magnifier, and toggle it on. Once activated, you can access the Magnifier quickly by triple-clicking the side button (or the Home button, depending on your model).

The Magnifier app offers a range of controls to adjust the zoom level, brightness, contrast, and even apply color filters, which can enhance readability for those with certain visual impairments, such as color blindness. It also allows you to freeze the frame to take a closer look at something without having to keep the device steady. This can be particularly helpful for tasks that require precision, like threading a needle or examining fine details in a document.

Display Zoom: Enhancing Overall Screen Visibility

Display Zoom is another powerful tool that increases the size of icons and text across the entire user interface of the iPhone 14. This feature is designed to make the screen easier to navigate for those who find the default settings too small or difficult to read. To activate Display Zoom, navigate to Settings > Display & Brightness > View, then select "Zoomed." This setting will scale up the interface, making everything from text messages to app icons larger and clearer.

The combination of Display Zoom with other text-sizing options available in the Accessibility settings allows users to customize their display to a level that suits their specific visual preferences. For users who struggle with visual fatigue or eye strain, these adjustments can make prolonged use of the iPhone more comfortable and sustainable.

Integration with Other Accessibility Features

Both Magnifier and Display Zoom can be used in conjunction with other accessibility features such as VoiceOver or Bold Text, providing a comprehensive suite of tools for users with visual impairments. This integration ensures that users can tailor their devices to meet a wide array of needs, enhancing their overall user experience.

By enabling and configuring Magnifier and Display Zoom on the iPhone 14, users with low vision can significantly enhance their ability to see and interact with their device. These features underscore Apple's commitment to accessibility, ensuring that every user can experience the full capabilities of their iPhone, regardless of their visual acuity.

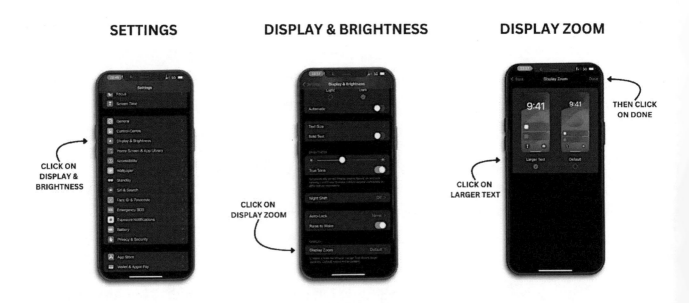

Customizing Your iPhone for Accessibility

Customizing the accessibility features on your iPhone 14 is crucial for creating a device experience that suits your unique needs, particularly if you have specific accessibility requirements. Apple's commitment to accessibility is evident in the wide array of customizable options available, designed to assist users with diverse abilities. This section will explore how you can tailor these features to enhance your interaction with your iPhone, making it more user-friendly and responsive to your individual preferences.

Accessing the Accessibility Menu

To begin customizing your iPhone for accessibility, navigate to the Settings app and select Accessibility. This menu is the control center for all accessibility features, offering options for vision, hearing, physical and motor skills, and more. Each category is thoughtfully designed to accommodate a wide range of needs, providing tools and adjustments that can significantly improve the usability of your device.

Customizable Vision Accommodations

For users with visual impairments, the iPhone 14 allows significant customization. Options such as text size and display settings can be adjusted to increase legibility. You can choose from a variety of color filters, reduce white point, or even invert colors to ensure optimal comfort for your eyes. Additionally, the Zoom function can be finely tuned to magnify any section of the screen in a resizable window, providing detailed visibility without losing context.

Adapting Audio and Visual Alerts

For those with hearing impairments, the iPhone 14 offers several ways to customize how you receive audio and visual alerts. You can set your phone to flash the LED light for alerts or use on-screen notification previews. Sound settings can be adjusted so that audio is directed to a preferred ear or enhanced to differentiate foreground sounds from background noise. These adjustments ensure that you won't miss important calls, messages, or alerts.

Physical and Motor Skills Adjustments

Users with limited physical or motor skills can customize their iPhone's touch settings to better suit their level of dexterity. Touch Accommodation adjusts how the screen responds to touch, allowing for longer duration before a touch is recognized, or ignoring repeated touches. AssistiveTouch can be customized to perform gestures like a pinch or multi-finger swipe with a single tap or a custom gesture, facilitating easier device use without the need for complex finger movements.

Voice Control and Dictation

Voice Control is an advanced feature that enables users to navigate their iPhone using voice commands. This feature can be finely adjusted to recognize specific vocal nuances, improving accuracy for users with unique speech patterns. Dictation allows for easy text entry by speaking directly to the device, which can be a game-changer for users with motor or vision impairments.

Creating Accessibility Shortcuts

Finally, Accessibility Shortcuts allow you to quickly turn on or off your favorite accessibility features with triple-clicks of the Home or Side button. You can set up shortcuts for features like VoiceOver, Magnifier, or Color Filters, making them readily accessible without having to navigate through settings menus each time.

By customizing these accessibility settings, your iPhone 14 becomes not just a tool, but a personalized support device that respects and responds to your individual needs. Whether enhancing visual, auditory, or physical interactions, the iPhone's extensive accessibility features ensure that all users can enjoy a seamless, inclusive mobile experience.

Conclusion to Chapter 8: Accessibility Features

The accessibility features integrated into the iPhone 14 exemplify Apple's dedication to inclusivity. Throughout this chapter, we have outlined how these tools not only aid in everyday tasks but also empower users by providing greater control over their device interaction. By exploring and customizing features such as VoiceOver, Magnifier, Display Zoom, and various tailor-made settings, users can enhance their experience to suit personal accessibility needs. The iPhone's built-in features are designed to accommodate a wide range of disabilities, ensuring that all users can benefit from the technology's full potential. As we conclude, remember that regularly exploring the Accessibility menu and updates from Apple can provide ongoing opportunities to improve how you interact with your iPhone. Embrace these tools to make your device a true assistant in navigating the digital world, proving that technology can be universally accessible and incredibly empowering.

Chapter 9: Troubleshooting Common Issues

Navigating the occasional hiccup with your iPhone 14 is an essential skill for any user, ensuring that minor issues don't disrupt your daily activities or degrade your overall experience. This chapter is dedicated to helping you understand and resolve some of the most common issues that you might encounter. From restarting and resetting your iPhone to troubleshooting Wi-Fi and cellular connection issues, managing storage space efficiently, and handling frozen apps and crashes, we've covered all the bases. Each section provides step-by-step instructions and practical advice designed to troubleshoot problems quickly and effectively. Whether you're a seasoned tech enthusiast or a new iPhone user, these tips will empower you to keep your device running smoothly, optimizing both its performance and your productivity.

Restarting and Resetting Your iPhone

When your iPhone 14 isn't behaving as expected, restarting or resetting the device can often resolve many common issues. This process can help clear up glitches by refreshing the system and closing apps that may not be running properly. This section explores the steps for both restarting and resetting your iPhone, ensuring you know how to safely and effectively handle these procedures when needed.

Restarting Your iPhone 14

Restarting your iPhone is a simple and quick solution that can fix minor bugs, such as apps crashing or the device running slowly. To restart your iPhone 14, press and hold the side button along with the volume up or down button until two sliding buttons appear. Drag the slider that says "slide to power off" to turn off your device. After the device turns off, press and hold the side button again until the Apple logo appears, indicating that your iPhone is rebooting.

This process does not affect your data or settings; it merely refreshes your operating system, which can often restore functionality to apps or system features that were previously malfunctioning.

Resetting Your iPhone 14

If restarting does not resolve the issue, you might consider resetting your iPhone. Resetting can refer to either a soft reset, which is similar to a restart but more thorough, or a hard reset, which restores the iPhone's settings to factory defaults.

- **Soft Reset:** This is effectively a more forceful restart. To perform a soft reset, press and quickly release the volume up button, then press and quickly release the volume down button. Finally, press and hold the side button until the screen turns off and the Apple logo appears, then release the button. This process can help resolve more persistent issues without erasing your data.

- **Hard Reset (Factory Reset):** This should be used as a last resort, as it will erase all data from your iPhone and restore it to its original settings. Before proceeding, ensure you have backed up all important data. To factory reset your iPhone, go to Settings > General > Reset and tap "Erase All Content and Settings." You will need to enter your passcode and confirm your decision. Once confirmed, the iPhone will begin erasing all data and settings, returning it to its original state.

It's important to differentiate between these options to choose the most appropriate solution for the issue you are experiencing. A restart or soft reset often resolves most problems, while a hard reset should only be used when absolutely necessary, as it removes all personal data from the device.

When to Use These Options

Choose to restart your iPhone when apps crash or the device is slower than usual. A soft reset can be useful if the device is unresponsive or peculiar behavior persists after a restart. A hard reset is recommended only if your iPhone is experiencing ongoing and unresolved issues that significantly affect its functionality, and you have backed up all necessary information.

Understanding how to properly restart or reset your iPhone is crucial for maintaining its performance and longevity. These troubleshooting steps can help keep your device running smoothly, ensuring you continue to enjoy the best user experience possible.

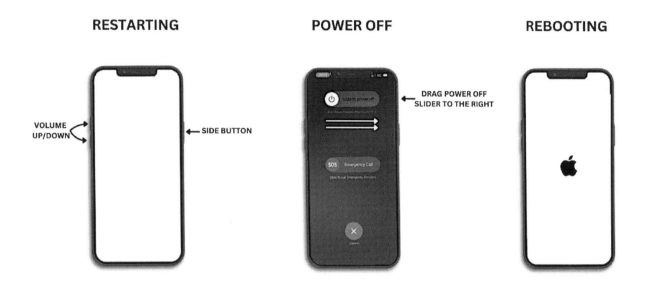

RESTARTING   POWER OFF   REBOOTING

VOLUME UP/DOWN

SIDE BUTTON

DRAG POWER OFF SLIDER TO THE RIGHT

Fixing Wi-Fi and Cellular Connection Issues

Experiencing difficulties with Wi-Fi or cellular connections on your iPhone 14 can be frustrating, especially when you rely on your device for daily communications, work, and access to information. This section provides detailed guidance on how to troubleshoot and resolve common connectivity issues, ensuring that your iPhone maintains a stable and reliable connection.

Troubleshooting Wi-Fi Connectivity

If your iPhone 14 is struggling to connect to Wi-Fi, or if the connection is unstable, start by ensuring your Wi-Fi router is online and functioning properly. Sometimes, the issue may be with the router rather than your iPhone. Restarting your router can resolve many network connectivity problems. If other devices can connect to the Wi-Fi network but your iPhone cannot, proceed with the following steps:

1. Toggle Wi-Fi Off and On: Sometimes, simply turning Wi-Fi off and then back on can resolve a connectivity issue. Go to Settings > Wi-Fi, and toggle it off and on.

2. Forget and Reconnect to the Network: Go to Settings > Wi-Fi, tap the information icon next to the network, and select "Forget This Network." After forgetting the network, reconnect by selecting it from the list of available networks and re-entering the password.

3. Check for iOS Updates: Sometimes, connectivity issues can be resolved by updating your iOS to the latest version, which often includes bug fixes and improvements for connectivity.

4. Reset Network Settings: If the issue persists, try resetting your network settings. Go to Settings > General > Reset > Reset Network Settings. This action will erase all network settings, returning them to factory defaults, and may solve your problem.

Addressing Cellular Data Issues

If you're experiencing issues with cellular data, such as slow speeds or no connectivity, consider the following steps to resolve the problem:

1. Check Carrier Settings Update: Make sure your carrier settings are up to date. Go to Settings > General > About, and if there's an update available, you'll receive a prompt to update your carrier settings.

2. Enable/Disable Airplane Mode: Quickly toggling Airplane Mode on and off can sometimes resolve cellular data issues. Swipe down from the top-right corner of your screen to open Control Center, and tap the airplane icon.

3. Reinsert SIM Card: Sometimes, removing and reinserting your SIM card can help restore cellular service as it re-establishes a connection with your network provider.

4. Contact Your Carrier: If you continue to have issues, there may be a problem with your account or network coverage. Contacting your carrier can help identify and resolve service issues or account-specific problems.

When to Seek Professional Help

If none of the above solutions restore your Wi-Fi or cellular connectivity, it may indicate a hardware problem with your iPhone 14. In such cases, it's advisable to contact Apple Support or visit an authorized service provider to diagnose and address potentially serious issues.

By following these troubleshooting steps, most connectivity problems with your iPhone 14 can be effectively resolved, allowing you to stay connected reliably and securely.

Managing Storage Space

In today's digital age, efficiently managing the storage space on your iPhone 14 is crucial to ensure smooth performance and adequate room for all your apps, photos, and other content. As you continue to use your device, storage can quickly fill up, leading to potential slowdowns and the inability to download new apps or updates. This section will guide you through several effective strategies to manage your iPhone's storage, helping you optimize space and maintain your device's functionality.

Checking Storage Usage

The first step in managing storage is to understand what is taking up space on your iPhone. To check your storage usage, go to Settings > General > iPhone Storage. Here, you'll see a bar graph breaking down how much space is being used by different categories such as apps, photos, media, and system data. Below the graph, you can see a list of apps and the amount of storage each one is using. This overview helps you identify potential areas for storage cleanup.

Offloading Unused Apps

iOS offers a convenient feature called Offload Unused Apps, which automatically removes apps you haven't used in a while but keeps their documents and data. This can free up space while allowing you to reinstall the app later without losing your data. To enable this feature, go to Settings > iTunes & App Stores and toggle on Offload Unused Apps. You can also manually offload individual apps by going to Settings > General > iPhone Storage, tapping on an app, and selecting Offload App.

Managing Photos and Videos

Photos and videos often consume a significant portion of iPhone storage. Optimizing this space can have a substantial impact. Consider enabling iCloud Photos to store your photos and videos in iCloud, keeping only smaller, space-saving versions on your device. To turn on iCloud Photos, go to Settings > Photos and toggle on iCloud Photos. Additionally, regularly review your photo library and delete any unnecessary or duplicate photos and videos.

Clearing Browser Cache and Data

Over time, your Safari browser can accumulate a lot of data and cache, which can also take up space. To clear Safari's cache, go to Settings > Safari and tap Clear History and Website Data. This not only frees up storage but can also speed up your browsing experience.

Deleting Old Messages and Attachments

Messages can accumulate significant amounts of data from texts, photos, and videos. You can set messages to automatically delete after a certain period. Go to Settings > Messages > Keep Messages, and select either 30 days or 1 year. This automatically deletes older messages, thereby managing storage space effectively. Additionally, review large attachments in Messages by going to Settings > General > iPhone Storage > Messages and tapping Review Large Attachments. Here, you can delete items that are no longer needed.

Regular Reviews and Cleanup

Regularly reviewing and cleaning your iPhone's storage can prevent it from becoming overburdened. Make it a routine to check your storage usage and clean out unnecessary files and apps. This proactive approach keeps your iPhone running efficiently and ensures you have enough space for important updates and new content.

By following these strategies, you can effectively manage your iPhone 14's storage space, enhancing its performance and longevity. Managing storage is not just about freeing up space— it's about optimizing your iPhone's functionality to suit your digital lifestyle.

Dealing with Frozen Apps and Crashes

Experiencing a frozen app or system crash can be frustrating, especially when it disrupts your workflow or personal use of your iPhone 14. Such issues can arise due to software glitches, memory problems, or app conflicts. This section outlines effective strategies to troubleshoot and resolve these common problems, ensuring your device operates smoothly and reliably.

Identifying the Problem App

The first step in addressing frozen apps or crashes is to identify the problematic app. If your iPhone freezes or crashes when using a specific app, that app is likely the culprit. Check for updates in the App Store for that app, as developers often release patches to fix bugs that could be causing the issue.

Force Quitting Frozen Apps

If an app becomes unresponsive, you should force quit the app:
1. On an iPhone with Face ID, swipe up from the bottom of the screen and pause in the middle of the screen. On an iPhone with a Home button, quickly double-click the Home button.
2. You will see all apps currently open in the app switcher. Swipe right or left to find the app you want to close.
3. Swipe up on the app's preview to close it.
After force quitting, reopen the app to see if it runs smoothly. If it continues to freeze, there may be deeper issues at play.

Restarting Your iPhone

If force quitting doesn't resolve the problem, or if your iPhone itself is unresponsive, a restart may be necessary. Restarting your device can clear out the memory that apps were using and gives a fresh start to the operating system. Press and hold the side button and either volume button (on Face ID models) until the power off slider appears. Drag the slider to turn off your iPhone, then press and hold the side button again to turn it back on.

Updating iOS

Running outdated software can sometimes lead to apps not functioning correctly. Check for an iOS update by going to Settings > General > Software Update. Installing updates can provide crucial fixes and improvements that may solve the problem.

Resetting iPhone Settings

If the crashes continue, consider resetting all settings on your iPhone. This action won't erase your data, but it will reset system settings such as Wi-Fi passwords and wallpaper. Go to Settings > General > Reset > Reset All Settings. This can resolve issues caused by incorrect or corrupt settings.

Reinstalling Problematic Apps

If a specific app is consistently problematic, try uninstalling and then reinstalling it. This can often clear up any corrupted data or settings associated with the app. To uninstall, press and hold the app icon, tap Remove App, and then tap Delete App. Reinstall it from the App Store.

Seeking Further Help

If your iPhone continues to experience frequent crashes or specific apps still freeze after following these steps, it may be useful to contact Apple Support or visit an Apple Store. There may be more complex issues with your device that require professional diagnosis and repair.

By systematically addressing frozen apps and crashes with these steps, you can often resolve minor issues yourself and restore optimal functionality to your iPhone 14, ensuring a smooth and enjoyable user experience.

Conclusion to Chapter 9: Troubleshooting Common Issues

Throughout this chapter, we have explored a variety of strategies to help you troubleshoot and resolve common issues that might arise with your iPhone 14. By understanding how to effectively restart and reset your device, fix connection problems, manage storage, and deal with unresponsive apps, you are now better equipped to maintain your iPhone's performance and extend its lifespan. Remember, most issues you'll encounter have simple solutions that can be implemented without needing professional help. However, if problems persist after following the guidance provided, it may be time to consult with Apple Support or visit an Apple Store for further assistance. Keeping your iPhone in good working order ensures that you can rely on it when you need it most, whether for work, entertainment, or staying connected with others.

Chapter 10: Advanced Tips and Tricks

As you become more familiar with your iPhone 14, you may find yourself eager to delve deeper into its capabilities and explore features that can significantly enhance your user experience. Chapter 10 is dedicated to unveiling those advanced tips and tricks that leverage the iPhone's cutting-edge technology. Here, we will guide you through a variety of sophisticated functionalities, including mastering multitasking, utilizing Siri for voice commands, customizing your home screen with widgets, and harnessing the power of shortcuts to streamline your daily activities. Each section is crafted to provide you with actionable insights that go beyond the basics, helping you to not only understand but also maximize the full potential of your iPhone. Whether for productivity, ease of use, or entertainment, these advanced tips and tricks will elevate your interaction with your device, making every swipe and tap more efficient and enjoyable.

Multitasking on Your iPhone

In today's fast-paced world, efficiency is key, and multitasking on your iPhone 14 can significantly enhance your productivity. Apple has designed the iPhone with powerful multitasking features that allow you to perform multiple tasks simultaneously without sacrificing performance. This section explores how to leverage these capabilities to make the most of your device, from using the App Switcher to Picture-in-Picture (PiP) mode, ensuring you can stay productive and connected no matter where you are.

Using the App Switcher

The App Switcher is an essential tool for multitasking on your iPhone. It allows you to quickly switch between apps or return to your most recently used apps without having to navigate back to the home screen. To access the App Switcher, swipe up from the bottom of the screen and pause in the middle of the screen if you're using an iPhone with Face ID. On models with a home button, quickly double-click the Home button. Here, you'll see previews of all open apps. Swipe left or right to find the app you want to switch to and tap it to bring it to the foreground.

Split View and Slide Over

While traditional split-screen multitasking is not available on iPhone, certain apps offer their own versions of multitasking. For example, some productivity apps allow you to open multiple documents or files at once within the app, emulating a Split View experience. Apps like Mail might let you manage your inbox while composing a message at the same time, which increases efficiency.

Picture-in-Picture (PiP) Mode

PiP mode is a game-changer for multitasking, particularly if you like to watch videos or take video calls. It allows you to minimize the video screen to a small, resizable window that floats over other apps. To use PiP, start playing a video and then press the Home button or swipe up to go Home, and the video will automatically scale down to a corner of your display. You can drag it to any corner, and tap the PiP window to control playback or close the video.

Interactive Notifications

Stay engaged with other tasks without missing important updates by using interactive notifications. You can respond to texts, emails, and calendar notifications directly from the lock screen or notification center. This feature lets you handle small tasks immediately, without having to fully open the respective apps.

Background App Refresh

This feature allows apps to update their content in the background while you work on other tasks. To manage this effectively, go to Settings > General > Background App Refresh. Here, you can choose which apps you want to refresh content in the background to ensure that they are up-to-date when you need them, while also conserving battery life by limiting background activity for apps you use less frequently.

By mastering these multitasking features, you can transform the way you use your iPhone, making it a more powerful tool for managing your daily tasks and activities efficiently. Whether you're switching between apps, interacting with notifications, or using PiP to continue watching a video while sending an email, your iPhone supports you in doing more in less time.

Using Siri for Voice Commands

Siri, Apple's voice-activated personal assistant, transforms how you interact with your iPhone 14 by allowing you to use voice commands to execute tasks effortlessly. This powerful tool not only enhances accessibility but also streamlines your daily activities, making technology more intuitive and responsive. In this section, we will explore how to maximize the capabilities of Siri to make your iPhone experience more efficient and personalized.

Activating Siri

First, ensure Siri is enabled on your iPhone 14. Go to Settings > Siri & Search, and toggle on "Listen for 'Hey Siri'," which allows you to activate Siri with just your voice when you say "Hey Siri." Alternatively, you can enable "Press Side Button for Siri" to activate Siri by pressing the side button.

Making Calls and Sending Messages

One of the most common uses of Siri is to make phone calls and send messages hands-free. Simply activate Siri and say, "Call [contact name]" or "Send a message to [contact name]." You can dictate the content of your message, and Siri will type and send it for you, making communication seamless and safe, especially when you're driving.

Setting Reminders and Calendar Events

Siri is incredibly useful for managing your schedule. You can ask Siri to set reminders for specific tasks like "Remind me to call John at 3 PM tomorrow" or "Remind me to buy milk when I leave work." Similarly, you can manage your calendar by saying, "Schedule a meeting with Lisa at noon next Friday." Siri integrates these directly into your iPhone's Reminders and Calendar apps, syncing across all your devices if you use iCloud.

Information and Entertainment

Siri can also serve as a source of information and entertainment. Ask Siri questions like "What's the weather like today?" or "How did the stock market do today?" and get instant replies. For entertainment, tell Siri to "Play my workout playlist" or "What are the latest NFL scores?" Siri can also control smart home devices if they are compatible with Apple HomeKit, allowing commands like, "Turn on the living room lights" or "Set the thermostat to 70 degrees."

Using Siri Shortcuts

For more advanced users, Siri Shortcuts allow you to create custom commands that automate a sequence of actions from different apps. For example, you can create a shortcut to send your daily arrival time to a family member, start a playlist, and get navigation directions to work with a single command like "Heading to work."

Customizing Siri's Responses

You can customize how Siri interacts with you by going to Settings > Siri & Search. Here, you can choose Siri's voice, language, and even toggle Siri responses between spoken feedback or text only, which is particularly useful in quiet environments.

By effectively utilizing Siri for voice commands, you transform your interaction with your iPhone 14, making it more engaging and suited to your lifestyle. Siri not only simplifies tasks but also enriches your iPhone experience, proving that voice can be the most natural way to interact with technology.

Customizing Widgets on Your Home Screen

Widgets have transformed the way users interact with their iPhone, offering a highly customizable and visually appealing interface to access real-time data and functionality right from the home screen. With the release of iOS 14 and subsequent updates, Apple has significantly enhanced widget capabilities on the iPhone 14, making them an essential component for personalizing your user experience. This section will guide you through customizing widgets on your home screen to improve both your iPhone's functionality and aesthetic.

Understanding Widgets

Widgets are mini-applications that run on your home screen, providing quick updates and easy access to a variety of features without needing to open the app itself. Whether it's the weather forecast, your calendar, fitness activity, or stock updates, widgets can keep you informed at a glance.

Adding Widgets to Your Home Screen

To begin customizing with widgets, press and hold any empty area on your home screen until the apps jiggle. Tap the plus icon in the upper-left corner to open the widget gallery. Here, you'll find an array of widgets from both Apple and third-party developers. Browse through the options and select a widget that you'd like to add. You can choose from different sizes, each offering varying levels of detail. Drag the chosen widget to your home screen or tap "Add Widget" and position it where you prefer.

Organizing Your Widgets

Efficient organization of your widgets is key to maximizing their utility. Place the widgets you check most frequently in positions where they are easily viewable upon unlocking your phone. For instance, if you're an avid scheduler, having the calendar widget at the top of your home screen can provide immediate access to your daily agenda. You can also stack widgets of the same size by dragging them on top of one another to create a scrollable stack. This not only saves space but also allows you to access multiple widgets in one spot.

Smart Stacks and Customization

One of the most powerful features is the Smart Stack, which uses on-device intelligence to surface the right widget based on time, location, and activity. You can create your own Smart Stack by manually stacking widgets or edit an existing one by adding or removing widgets from the stack. This feature is ideal for users who prefer a dynamic home screen that adapts throughout the day.

Personalizing Widget Content

Many widgets allow you to further personalize the content they display. For example, you can customize the Photos widget to cycle through a particular album or set the News widget to show stories from your favorite categories or sources. To customize, tap and hold the widget and select "Edit Widget" to access its settings.

Utility and Aesthetics

While widgets are highly functional, they also offer aesthetic enhancements to your home screen. Choosing the right color scheme and layout that complements your wallpaper and icons can make your iPhone visually pleasing and uniquely yours.

By mastering the use of widgets and understanding how to customize them effectively, you can significantly enhance your iPhone experience. Widgets not only provide efficiency by delivering information at a glance but also allow you to express your style and preferences directly on your home screen.

Exploring Shortcuts for Efficiency

The Shortcuts app on your iPhone 14 is a powerful tool that automates complex tasks, turning them into simple actions that can be executed with a tap or via Siri. This feature is particularly useful for streamlining your daily activities, enhancing both productivity and your device's functionality. In this section, we will delve into how to effectively use and customize shortcuts to maximize your efficiency and make your interaction with your iPhone more fluid and intuitive.

Understanding Shortcuts

Shortcuts are essentially quick actions across your apps and features that are automated through the Shortcuts app. These can range from sending a scheduled text message to starting a playlist and navigating to a specific location without manually opening multiple apps or performing several steps. The beauty of shortcuts lies in their customization and flexibility, allowing you to tailor actions to your lifestyle and needs.

Creating a Shortcut

To create a new shortcut, open the Shortcuts app and tap the "+" button. You will enter the creation screen where you can search for actions or select from a list. For instance, if you want to create a shortcut to send a daily greeting message to a friend, you can add actions to send a message via the Messages app and schedule this shortcut to run at a specific time each day.

Using the Gallery

For those new to shortcuts or seeking inspiration, the Shortcuts Gallery is an excellent starting point. It features a curated collection of ready-made shortcuts that can be added to your library with just a tap. These range from productivity boosters to shortcuts designed for health, lifestyle, and entertainment. Exploring the gallery can provide ideas on how shortcuts can fit into various aspects of your digital routine.

Integrating with Siri

Shortcuts can be integrated with Siri to enhance hands-free operation. Each shortcut can be assigned a unique phrase that when spoken to Siri, triggers the action. This integration proves incredibly useful for tasks you perform regularly or when you need to execute actions while on the move, such as starting a navigation route or sending your estimated time of arrival to a contact.

Advanced Shortcuts with Multiple Steps

For more advanced users, shortcuts can be created with multiple steps from different apps. For example, you can create a shortcut that pulls up your top news, weather forecast, and daily calendar agenda with a single command each morning. By combining multiple actions into one shortcut, you streamline your day's start effectively and efficiently.

Sharing and Syncing Shortcuts

Shortcuts can be shared with friends or synced across multiple iOS devices, ensuring you have access to your customized actions no matter which device you are using. This sharing is straightforward through iCloud, making it easy to maintain consistency in your automated tasks across your Apple devices.

By exploring and utilizing the Shortcuts app, you transform your iPhone into a more capable and customized tool. Whether simplifying daily tasks, optimizing complex sequences, or integrating with Siri for voice-activated controls, shortcuts elevate your iPhone's operational efficiency to new heights.

Conclusion to Chapter 10: Advanced Tips and Tricks

Throughout this chapter, we've explored a range of advanced functionalities that your iPhone 14 offers, designed to enrich your interaction with technology and enhance your daily digital experience. From multitasking more effectively to personalizing voice commands with Siri, optimizing your home screen with dynamic widgets, and creating powerful shortcuts, these tips and tricks unlock new levels of productivity and customization. By implementing these advanced features, you can tailor your iPhone to better suit your lifestyle and needs, making it a truly indispensable tool. As technology continues to evolve, so too will the capabilities of your iPhone, and staying abreast of these advancements will ensure that you continue to benefit from the most innovative and useful features available. We encourage you to revisit these tips regularly and experiment with new ways to use your iPhone as more features and updates become available, keeping your experience both fresh and rewarding.

HOME SCREEN   **SHORTCUTS**   **ADD ACTION**

CLICK ON
SHORTCUT ICON

CLICK ON
+ ICON

ADD ACTION

CLICK
DONE

ACTION
SUGGESTION LIST

Conclusion

Congratulations on Becoming an iPhone 14 Expert!

As you conclude this journey through the comprehensive guide to mastering your iPhone 14, take a moment to reflect on the breadth of knowledge you've acquired. From understanding the basic functionalities to exploring advanced features, you have equipped yourself with the skills to navigate your device like a true expert. The capabilities of the iPhone 14 are vast, and your ability to utilize them fully can significantly enhance not only your personal productivity but also your digital enjoyment.

This guide has walked you through essential setups, daily operations, troubleshooting common issues, and leveraging the iPhone's extensive features for multitasking and personalization. You've learned to manage settings that enhance the device's security and privacy, ensuring that you maintain control over your digital footprint. Additionally, the integration of Siri and the customization of your home screen with widgets have hopefully transformed your interaction with the iPhone, making it more tailored and intuitive.

By now, you should feel confident in your ability to handle a variety of tasks and resolve any challenges that may arise. The journey to becoming proficient with your iPhone 14 is an ongoing process of exploration and adaptation. As iOS updates are released and new apps are developed, new possibilities will open up, offering even more ways to enhance your experience.

Remember, the true expertise in technology comes not only from understanding how to use a device but also from knowing how to make the device work for you. Embrace the continuous learning curve, and keep experimenting with new features and settings. Your iPhone is a powerful tool that, when mastered, can be an invaluable companion in your everyday life.

Further Resources for Ongoing Learning

Embracing the full potential of your iPhone 14 involves continuous learning and adaptation. As technology evolves, so do the opportunities to enhance your understanding and skills. To ensure you remain adept and informed, consider engaging with a variety of resources designed to keep you updated and proficient with your iPhone.

Apple's Support Website provides an extensive library of articles and tutorials that cover every aspect of your iPhone. From basic operations to advanced settings, this resource is invaluable for both troubleshooting and discovering new features.

Online Forums and Communities such as Apple's official discussion boards or other tech forums offer a place to share information, ask questions, and learn from experienced users. These communities are often among the first to explore new updates and find innovative uses for iPhone features.

YouTube Channels and Tech Blogs offer tutorials, reviews, and tips that can enhance your understanding and use of the iPhone. These platforms often provide visual and practical guides that are easy to follow and implement.

Books and eBooks on iPhone use and tips are also valuable resources. They provide comprehensive guides that you can refer to at your convenience. These texts often range from beginner to advanced levels, ensuring there is something for every stage of your learning journey.

Workshops and Training Sessions can also be beneficial, especially those offered by Apple in their retail stores. These sessions are tailored to help you get more from your iPhone, with expert guidance in a hands-on learning environment.

By utilizing these resources, you ensure that your knowledge remains current and that you continue to leverage the iPhone's capabilities fully. Keep exploring, learning, and adapting, and your experience with the iPhone 14 will only grow richer with time.

Made in the USA
Columbia, SC
13 October 2024

44216765R00063